Dare We Speak of God in Public?

Dare We Speak of God in Public?

The Edward Cadbury Lectures, 1993–94

Edited by Frances Young

MOWBRAY

Mowbray
A Cassell imprint
Villiers House, 41/47 Strand, London WC2N 5JE

387 Park Avenue South
New York
NY 10016-8810

First published 1995

British Library Cataloguing-in-Publication Data
A catalogue record for this book is available from the British Library.

ISBN 0-264-67366-2

Printed and bound in Great Britain by
Biddles Ltd, Guildford and King's Lynn

Contents

The Contributors

Rex Ambler is Lecturer in Theology at the University of Birmingham

David F. Ford is Regius Professor of Divinity in the University of Cambridge

John Hull is Professor of Religious Education at the University of Birmingham

Gareth Jones is Lecturer in Theology at the University of Birmingham

Paul Joyce is Lecturer in Biblical Studies at the University of Oxford and Fellow of St Peter's College

Emmanuel Lartey is Lecturer in Pastoral Studies at the University of Birmingham

Hugh McLeod is Professor of Church History at the University of Birmingham

Stephen Pattison is Lecturer in the School of Health, Welfare and Community Education at the Open University and Honorary Lecturer in the Department of Theology at the University of Birmingham

Werner Ustorf is Professor of Mission at the University of Birmingham and Selly Oak Colleges

Isabel Wollaston is Lecturer in Theology at the University of Birmingham

Frances Young is Edward Cadbury Professor of Theology at the University of Birmingham

Preface

The Edward Cadbury Lectureship Endowment provides for an annual series of eight public lectures in the University of Birmingham on some aspect of the Christian religion. These are usually given by a distinguished visiting scholar. In 1993–94, however, a perhaps fortunate mischance left a gap in the programme of invitees. One of our number suggested that we should 'do our own thing'.

The idea grew, and the subject suggested itself. We spoke as a group of theologians working on an explicitly secular campus and increasingly conscious of the pluralist, post-Christian world which is our context. The eight lectures were delivered by current members of the staff of Birmingham University's Department of Theology, together with John Hull, Professor of Religious Education in the same university's School of Education. We were encouraged by the presence and support of new colleagues appointed after the initial planning – the series was very much a team event, facilitating mutual appreciation of the various different aspects of the subject we represent.

This book is the result, and we are proud that it joins a considerable collection of publications resulting from the Edward Cadbury Endowment. The eight lectures appear here written up, somewhat reordered, and joined by two additional pieces, one from Stephen Pattison, formerly Pastoral Studies Lecturer in the Birmingham Theology Department and now of the Open University, and one from Paul Joyce, who happened to be away on study leave at the time of the lecture series. In addition we have invited David Ford, now Regius Professor of Divinity in the University of Cambridge but formerly one of our colleagues as Lecturer in Theology in Birmingham, to provide a concluding response to the collection of papers.

We acknowledge with gratitude the support of the Edward Cadbury Trust, and especially their willingness to encourage uses of the endowment not strictly envisaged in the original trust provisions; also, the contribution of the School of Continuing Studies in publicizing the event, the secretarial assistance of Mrs Margaret Egginton, and the support of our faithful audience. In addition we thank Judith Longman of Mowbray for her interest and encouragement.

Frances Young
Edward Cadbury Professor of Theology
University of Birmingham
May 1994

Introduction

It is well known that Government circles in the 1980s insisted that religion should be kept out of politics, consigning it to the sphere of private morality and personal faith. Probably the vast majority of people in our society, believers and non-believers alike, treat religion in such terms: it is a matter of individual choice or temperament, and has no bearing on public or professional life. In a pluralist society, tolerance and respect are seen as appropriate for the adherents of different religious positions: but the generally accepted fact is that religion is irrelevant, indeed potentially divisive, unable to contribute to the apprehension of truth about the way things are, and so best bracketed out of the machinery that deals with the public interest.

This state of affairs can be illustrated by two incidents. Ten years ago, the President of the Methodist Conference was addressing a group of persons about to be ordained as ministers: he suggested that they were on the point of being given a licence to speak of God in public, and articulated the widespread feeling that God is not a subject easily broached in casual conversation or public discourse in modern Britain. More recently, a Catholic layman was heard to suggest that talking about God was as embarrassing as talking about sex. Most people simply do not find it easy to talk about God, no matter how profound their own sense of God's reality, or their belief in the efficacy of prayer. For many, indeed, the idea of God's reality is surrounded by deep doubt and uncertainty, if not hostility, not least because God appears to have no effect in the world, a world riven by natural and moral, collective and individual evils.

On the other hand, many churchpeople regard social responsibility as an inherent part of their religious commitment, and feel frustrated that public life is so little responsive to the imperatives of Christian values. Liberation theology has made theology political throughout the globe. Politics has demonstrably been driven by religious motivations, among others, in some recent dramatic political transformations, such as those in eastern Germany and South Africa. Despite marginalization in Britain, language about God can still provide public validation of action and policy elsewhere.

In this book, the contributors seek to explore and analyse the present situation, discussing reasons, some of them cogent, why 'God-language' has become problematic and theology sidelined: but also, in many cases, endeavouring to show that there is life in the subject yet, and that talk of God still has a contribution to make in many contexts, if only people would listen. Each contributor speaks from the area of their own expertise, so that it may seem there is little in common, and little real dialogue going on. There is, indeed, a great variety in terms of both style and content, and readers may wish to dip around, and pick and choose. Nevertheless, the diversity is not without some unity of focus and some interesting convergences. What follows in this introduction is intended to provide a brief map, drawing out the sequence, and making some connections.

The opening chapter, from Hugh McLeod, puts a historical perspective on the present situation in England. It draws an effective contrast between the public profile and widespread influence of Christianity in the early years of this century and the rapid decline that has occurred since the 1950s, but at the same time challenges some easy assumptions about the privatization of religion.

In the order presented here, this is immediately followed by two chapters concerned with the place of religion and the contribution of theology in public education institutions. John Hull provides a highly topical piece offering a critique of recent legislation and Government circulars dealing with religious education and, in particular, collective worship in schools. There follows a personal and provocative statement from Stephen Pattison on theology as a university discipline, analysing both its ghetto status and its potential contribution to understanding society, human behaviour and public discourse. Maintaining the practical focus, consideration is then given to the place of religious language and analysis in psychotherapy, as Emmanuel Lartey enquires about 'God' in the couch.

The focus then shifts to questions raised for modern people about how to respond to religious texts and traditions, how they are to be interpreted, whether they are to be appropriated or rejected. Is there an insuperable gap between traditional religious expression and modern experience, which makes continued public discourse with shared assumptions impossible? Paul Joyce follows Emmanuel Lartey's piece by discussing readings of Scripture in the light of modern psychology, so providing an example of how general public discourse influences methods of interpretation. Isabel Wollaston then examines the continuities and discontinuities in Jewish religious language after the Holocaust.

That subject raises the question 'Where is God?'; for discourse about God has to face the distrust of a public perhaps more aware than ever before of disaster. Rex Ambler pursues further the question of where God is, especially in the light of the ecological crisis. Might that crisis not be a catalyst for the destruction of idols, and commitment to a God who 'lures us into becoming what we have it in us to become'? His emphasis on religion as enhancing freedom and responsibility coheres with much that Emmanuel Lartey explores earlier in the book.

Werner Ustorf wonders who finds it difficult to speak of God in public and why. He suggests a need for liberation from cultural certainties, an admission of ignorance so that religious experience and everyday experience may become revelatory. His voices 'from the backyard of history', ranging from Augustine and Ignatius of Loyola to twentieth-century non-European figures like Fukuoka of Japan and Kimbangu of the Congo, present a challenge to theologians who no longer dare to speak directly of God.

Two succeeding contributions, from Gareth Jones and the editor, draw on Christian theology, in both ancient and modern contexts, to explore questions concerning truth and prayer. Both stress the incompleteness of human knowledge of God, and yet show, among other things, the effectiveness of traditional Trinitarianism in enabling discourse about, or communication with, God. A note of coherence with several other contributions is found in the refusal to limit or demystify that which transcends human understanding, so presenting a creative dialectic between the necessarily agnostic relativism of contingent beings and a realism which affirms a God worthy of our faith, hope and worship, even in the context of modern evils, uncertainties and cultural diversities.

At the end, David Ford's chapter initiates discussion of all the collected material.

1
The privatization of religion in modern England

Hugh McLeod

England's modern religious history begins in 1689 with the Act of Toleration. This indicated that the State had given up the attempt to force Anglicanism on the whole population through compulsory church attendance and the persecution of rival denominations. It was followed in 1694 by the abolition of censorship, after which the publication of a series of deist works made London for a time the international centre of religious heterodoxy. The religious history of the period since 1689 might be seen in terms of a three-cornered contest between official religion, unofficial religion and secularism, in which the three combatants fought for influence over a fourth group – perhaps the largest of all – comprising those who had no such settled religious convictions.

When we speak of a 'privatization' of religion in the present century, I think we mean that religious language, religiously-based assumptions about the nature of the world and religiously-legitimated moral principles have become the preserve of committed minorities, rather than being part of the taken-for-granted assumptions of the majority of the population. Taken-for-granted assumptions are by their nature things that have not been reflected upon very deeply, and they are very often inconsistent with other taken-for-granted assumptions. They are highly vulnerable to changes in the mental atmosphere. The taken-for-granted assumptions of one generation can easily appear as absurdities to the next generation – this has happened many times during our religious history, and it has happened again during the last few decades.

I am going to begin with a brief historical overview of the three-sided contest that I have just mentioned, before focusing on the late Victorian and Edwardian period, when Christianity did still provide the basis for a common language accepted by the majority of the people. I shall then look at how far and why this situation has changed during the present century.

In the eighteenth century, the sceptics were making headway in the middle and upper classes while having little influence over the masses. That century saw its own process of religious privatization – though admittedly on a much more limited scale than in our own times. Religious zeal was labelled 'enthusiasm' and was certainly not for public display. God was renamed 'The Supreme Being'. (This process went much further in Revolutionary France, where 'fanatic' became the code word for 'practising Catholic', and 'mummery' a widely used term for Catholic ritual.) Bishop Butler wrote in 1736, no doubt with deliberate hyperbole:

> It is come, I know not how, to be taken for granted by many persons that Christianity is not so much a subject of inquiry, but that it is now at length discovered to be fictitious. And accordingly they treat it as if, in the present age, this were an agreed point among all people of discernment, and nothing remained but to set it up as a principal subject of mirth and ridicule, as it were by way of reprisals, for it having so long interrupted the pleasures of the world.[1]

When the tide turned in the 1790s, the immediate trigger was the French Revolution, which terrified monarchs, aristocrats and the wealthy generally in all parts of Europe, and created an atmosphere in which conservative politicians could mount a very effective 'back to basics' campaign.[2] This was only one among several factors leading to a dramatic change in the mental climate at this time. With the Romantic Movement in literature and art, enthusiasm was once again becoming socially acceptable. And, most important of all, the social and demographic upheavals associated with the beginnings of industrialization created a situation that was energetically exploited by Methodist and Dissenting evangelists.[3] In the early nineteenth century, official religion moved right back into fashion among the upper and upper middle classes, while unofficial religion was growing spectacularly among the lower middle and working classes. At the same time, scepticism, which was losing ground at the top of the social hierarchy, was making some inroads at the bottom. The stage was thus set for the religious drama of Victorian England, a period when established religion, dissenting religion and secularism were all highly organized, vocal and militant, and religious questions were always somewhere near to the top of the public agenda.[4]

Organized free-thought reached its numerical peak in the 1880s, and the same may well be true for organized Christianity; though this is hard to judge, since although we have plenty of statistics for Nonconformity, there are few statistics in this period for Anglicanism, and even fewer for Roman Catholicism.[5] Since the 1880s, a renewed process of religious privatization has set in. This time the process has affected all social classes, but it has been very gradual, and it is still far from complete. During this time, organized religion and organized free-thought have declined in tandem with one another. Although the influence of religious sceptics has increased, it is no longer to any significant degree exercised through anti-religious organizations.

The 1880s and 1890s saw changes in the mental atmosphere as far-reaching and many-sided as those that had taken place three generations earlier. Intellectual changes which had begun some years before were only now making a widespread impact. In particular, Darwinism and the declining credibility of the literalist approach to the Bible were making it harder than it had been to believe in Christianity, and easier than it had been to be an atheist or agnostic. Equally important were the political upheavals of the time. Social hierarchies of every kind were under attack. The movements for the emancipation of the working class and of women were gathering force, and many of the fighters in these causes were denouncing mainstream Christianity as an accomplice of the powers that be. Most far-reaching of all, though least understood, were the cultural changes of this period. The puritanism of the nineteenth century was under general attack. Contemporaries liked to rail against 'cant', 'rant' and 'humbug', and to proclaim the new watchwords of 'freedom' and 'individual self-development'.[6]

During the first half of the present century, the trend towards the increasing privatization of religion was very gradual, but the process has greatly accelerated since the 1960s. This period has seen a sharp decline in the strength of what I have termed 'official' religion, which by now may be said to include not only Anglicanism, but also Methodism and Roman Catholicism. At the same time, there has been a considerable growth both in the number of convinced unbelievers, and also in various new forms of dissenting religion, ranging from Islam and Hinduism, to charismatic house churches, to black Pentecostalism, to Jehovah's Witnesses, to New Age beliefs.[7] From the point of view of our present theme, however, it is important to note that, numerous as these latter groups are, their impact on public discourse has been very limited. The number of convinced religious believers may not have dropped very far, but it is the religious bodies in the social mainstream that have declined, while those that are most socially marginal have grown. For instance, these growing religious groups have little influence on politics, the media, or education, areas where the 'mainstream' churches were once very influential, and still have some influence.

* * *

So much for the historical overview. In the next section I am going to focus on the period from about 1880 until 1914, which was, maybe, the last time when someone could refer to England as a 'Christian country' without too much fear of contradiction. I shall try to explore the ways in which Christianity provided a common language that served in many different areas of life and was accepted, and to a large extent taken for granted, by the majority of the population. I am certainly not claiming that the majority of the population were deeply committed believers; but it was a measure of the success achieved by the Christian revival of the early nineteenth century that a certain minimum of Christian doctrine, ethics and ritual observance had become a normal part of life, though not necessarily a very large part of life, for anyone who had not made a conscious decision to reject them.[8] I shall explore some of the dimensions of this situation.

A first point is that the great majority of children were given a deliberately Christian upbringing. Whether or not parents participated directly in the religious education of their children, nearly all sent them to church and/or Sunday School, and after 1880 compulsory education meant that the great majority of children were also getting religious teaching in day school. As a result, it seems highly probable that a basic knowledge of Christian doctrine and ethical teaching was held by a higher proportion of the population during this period than at any other time before or since.[9] Some people deliberately rejected the religious upbringing that they were given, and many others remained fairly indifferent. But it seems that most of the latter remained at least passive believers.

The most basic and widely prevalent expression of this often fairly passive belief was the general acceptance of some kind of sectarian identity.[10] In parts of Lancashire, nearly everyone was conscious of being either Protestant or Catholic; in most other parts of the country, the division between church and chapel was equally generally recognized. Both kinds of division were reinforced by differences in employment patterns: many employers preferred workers of their own denomination. The Protestant–Catholic divide was the deeper. It was a form of tribal loyalty, reinforced by the use of derogatory nicknames and by a strong prejudice against intermarriage. The hostility between church and chapel was less. Yet there were profound cultural differences between them. Most obviously, they voted differently: church people voted Conservative, while chapel people voted Liberal, or sometimes Labour. But often there were differences in lifestyle and values. Church people were more likely to enjoy a guilt-free pint or a bet on the horses; they were more likely to be fervent patriots and monarchists, and more likely to be respectful of authority generally.

If, as I have said, Christianity provided a language that was understood, and to some extent used, by the majority of the population, the most obvious example of this was the use of the Christian rites of passage at the great turning-points of life. When a couple decided to marry, when a child was born to them, and when one of them died, it was in most cases the Anglican church which provided the rituals with which they marked the solemnity of each occasion, and expressed their joy or their sorrow. (It should be noted, incidentally, that the birth of a child was generally followed not only by the baptism of the child, but also by the churching of the mother.) The significance of these ceremonies was buried deep in the popular consciousness. In the eyes of many, a mother who went out before she was churched was unclean, an unbaptized baby was a little heathen, and a couple who had been married in a register office were living in sin.[11]

The role of Christianity in the mourning of the dead was observable not only in the funerals of ordinary people, but also in the mass mourning that followed the deaths of famous men and women, mining and shipping disasters, or deaths in war. Going forward a few years to 1919, it is notable that the cross, often combined with a biblical text, became absolutely standard in war memorials, in spite of the many alternatives that were tried in other traditionally Christian countries – for instance, in France the imagery was predominantly patriotic, and in Australia the favourite form of memorial was a soldier, gun in hand.[12]

At life's great turning-points, or at times of crisis, it was Christian language that best expressed most people's hopes and fears, and at such times many people prayed who otherwise gave God little thought. For instance, we have accounts of British soldiers praying before going into battle in World War I, or taking Communion while at the front, in the belief that they would thereby enjoy a period of immunity from bullets.[13]

The area of life where religion was perhaps most visible on a day-to-day basis was the education system. Robert Tressell, in his caustic novel of Edwardian working-class life, *The Ragged Trousered Philanthropists*, observed that all his characters, however slight their own religious convictions, agreed that 'Religion was a nice thing to teach children'.[14] And certainly, at every level from elementary school to university, religious teaching and/or religious personnel played a conspicuous part. Until the Education Act of 1870, elementary education was dominated by religious bodies, notably the Anglican National Society, and Anglican and Roman Catholic schools continued to play a large, albeit declining, role in elementary education, especially in Lancashire.[15] But even the Board Schools provided non-sectarian Bible teaching, and observers in the period around 1900 claimed that a high proportion of Board School teachers were active members of church or chapel.[16] Meanwhile, the children of the wealthy were educated in public schools, where the most conspicuous building was the chapel, the headmaster was very often a clergyman, and sermons were his preferred means of inculcating the prevailing ethos of patriotism and public service. Archbishops William Temple and Geoffrey Fisher were only the most recent examples of the many Anglican ecclesiastics who began their careers by teaching in public schools.[17] Even at university level, Oxford and Cambridge were only beginning to emerge from their past as specifically, and indeed until recently exclusively, Anglican institutions, and, for instance, chapel attendance remained compulsory until World War I.[18]

While the laws of Victorian and Edwardian England partly reflected ideas of Christian morality, a complex set of factors played a part here. For one thing, there was not always a consensus as to what Christian morality required, and even where such a consensus existed, views differed as to how far the State should go in enforcing such standards, or what other considerations should also play a part. There were also conflicts between the ethics generally upheld by Christian moralists and the actual practice of the upper-class and upper middle-class males who ran the country. For instance, Christian morality clearly prescribed marital fidelity for both sexes, but men in many social milieux, and most notably in the aristocracy, believed in the principle of a double standard.[19] A good example of the resulting tensions is offered by the famous, or infamous, Contagious Diseases Acts. These were prompted by the prevalence of venereal disease in the British Army and Navy, a problem that legislators proposed to remedy by compulsory medical inspections of women believed to be prostitutes who lived in certain military towns, such as Aldershot, Plymouth and Portsmouth. At the time, these attracted little attention, but within a few years they were the subject of a repeal campaign mounted in crusading style by a group of women motivated by a mixture of Christianity and feminism. The Christians especially objected to the fact that the State seemed to be condoning prostitution, and the feminists especially emphasized the discrimination implicit in the fact that it was the women rather than the soldiers who were subjected to the medical checks. Josephine Butler, the campaign's charismatic leader, who was a Christian feminist, objected on both grounds, and enjoyed considerable support from ministers of religion, predominantly Nonconformist. The crusade succeeded, and in 1886 the Acts were repealed. In this instance, the Christian moralists eventually triumphed — but Christian morality was far from being the only, or the first, consideration in the minds of legislators.[20] In some areas where the views of most Christian moralists conflicted with the practice of most upper-class males, legislators responded to demands for reform by concentrating their attack on the vices of the lower social classes. Thus, in the case of gambling, on-course betting, practised mainly by the wealthy, remained legal, whereas the Street Betting Act of 1906 attempted to suppress the street bookie, patronized by working-class men and women.[21]

What is left of all this? Convinced believers continue to use religious language — at least among themselves. Convinced sceptics reject it. The battleground lies in the middle. In the late Victorian period, Christian influences on this middle group were still strong. Since then, Christian influences have weakened but without any coherent alternative taking their place. The result is a considerable degree of confusion. In some areas of life the privatization of religion has continued apace; in some areas Christianity does continue to offer something of a common language, acceptable at least to those who are not convinced unbelievers; and in others something of a compromise has been reached.

In so far as the privatization of religion has taken place, why has it happened? Two major factors, as well as several minor factors, can be mentioned. The first major factor has been the growing pluralism of English society. The crucial point here has been not so much the immigration of Muslims, Hindus and Sikhs, as the growing number of alternatives to Christian belief among the nominally Christian population. This process goes back to the later nineteenth century, which saw not only the emergence of agnosticism and atheism as important options, but also the development of new forms of religious faith, such as Spiritualism and Theosophy. The second major factor has been professionalization — the emergence and local dominance of a series of professional groups, each enjoying a high degree of autonomy, and each with its own distinctive value-system and specialized language and its claims to exclusive authority within its own sphere. These have, in particular, the function of excluding any claims to jurisdiction by the church. This theme is of course a very old one, going back at least to the church–State conflicts of the medieval period. The modern period, however, has seen the battle refought on a smaller scale within many professions.

Among the minor factors has been the distinctive pattern of development in the relationship between religion and politics in twentieth-century Britain. In a number of Continental countries, the later nineteenth and early twentieth centuries saw a polarization between a Catholic Right and an anti-clerical Left. The result was that religious issues were continuously close to the top of the political agenda. Right-wing politicians rallied their supporters by appealing to their Catholicism, and left-wing politicians rallied their supporters by denouncing the clergy. In Britain, however, where, after World

War I, all parties contained a mixture of religious groups, all had an interest in avoiding religious controversies which might divide their own supporters.[22]

I next want to look at changes in various areas of religious life during this century. The most dramatic change has been the drastic decline suffered by Sunday Schools since World War II. In the later Victorian period, Sunday School enrolment peaked at slightly over 50 per cent of the population aged under 15. In 1931, it was still 46 per cent. But by 1951, it had dropped to 30 per cent and in 1989 it was only 7 per cent.[23] Up until World War II, Sunday School was a normal part of childhood, even for those whose parents had little connection with a church or chapel. A combination of factors contributed to this situation: Sunday Schools were a convenient way of getting children out of the house; they offered treats which the children themselves looked forward to; children needed to grow up with some basic religious knowledge, and they needed to know the difference between right and wrong. Sunday School, it was hoped, would help to give them these things.[24] Now all this has changed. Sunday School, instead of being a normal part of childhood, has become largely restricted to a Christian subculture. Those children whose parents are churchgoers will normally be in Sunday School while their parents are in church. Those whose parents do not go to church are unlikely to go at all. TV has taken over as the great child-minder. With rising living standards most parents can afford their own treats, and no longer need those provided by Sunday Schools. Perhaps most important, but most elusive, is the change in the religious atmosphere. Religiously uncommitted parents once tended to accept that England was a Christian country whose citizens needed to grow up knowing something about Christianity. Relatively few people now think this – and in any case they might well argue that the religious education provided in day school is sufficient. The problem of how to teach children the difference between right and wrong remains, but few people now think that Sunday Schools can make an important contribution to this.

The decline in the proportion of babies being christened follows a similar pattern. The decline is in fact very recent, but it is nonetheless dramatic. Throughout the first half of this century, the proportion of babies receiving an Anglican baptism oscillated around the two-thirds mark, and in 1950 it was still 67 per cent. Since then, however, there has been a steady decline, and the latest figure is 29 per cent.[25] The reasons for this decline are varied: immigration by non-Christians from south Asia, or of non-Anglican Christians from Ireland, Africa, the Caribbean and the Mediterranean; the more restrictive policies applied by some clergy. (I remember reading of a Chelmsley Wood couple who, when told by their vicar that they would have to attend church every Sunday for a month if they wanted their child christened, decided to do the job themselves – presumably they did not get into the statistics.) But the most important factor is that non-church-going parents no longer feel much social pressure to have their child christened – and many of them feel it would be hypocritical to do so.

Yet it should be noted that many non-church-going couples still do have their children christened. The 29 per cent of births that are followed by an Anglican baptism far exceed the 5 per cent or so of adults who are church-going Anglicans. Clearly, this particular Christian rite does still meet a vital need for a far wider section of the population than those who are committed church-members – though in this instance it is not so easy to say what the vital need is. The most basic factor, perhaps, is that the birth of a child is an event of momentous significance, perhaps the most moving experience that most people ever go through; and it therefore demands to be celebrated in a way commensurate with the dignity of the occasion. Many people may be unsure that the Anglican ceremony provides what they are looking for. But as yet there are no effective secular competitors – the choice for most people is between a Christian rite and none at all.

I shall return to this theme later. There are a number of areas of life in which Christian language no longer carries the general acceptance that it once enjoyed, but no widely accepted alternative language has yet been found.

One other area in which religion once entered into the lives of the great majority of the population, but no longer does so, is that of the defining of identity. I referred earlier to the great importance in Victorian and Edwardian England of the divisions between church and chapel and between Catholic and Protestant, and I mentioned the fact that this sense of religious identity was felt even by most of those who took no active part in any religious community. Two things have changed since then. One is that there is a much larger proportion of the population – about a quarter, according to public opinion polls – claiming no religious label at all.[26] But even for the majority who do acknowledge some label, there are relatively few for whom it plays any important part in shaping the way in which they see themselves. Indeed the most common religious label, 'C of E', often means no more than an assertion of normality and a desire to distance oneself from any kind of religious or irreligious zeal.[27] The only denominational distinction which still has some social significance is that between Protestant and Catholic. Catholics still have enough distinctive symbols, beliefs, loyalties, associations, to give them a sense of being different from everybody else – even if they themselves may be ambivalent about their heritage.[28] And most Protestants still retain some degree of suspicion of Catholicism and prejudice against

Catholics. It should be noted, however, that there have historically been two forms of anti-Catholicism in this country – one evangelical Protestant, which highlighted Catholic idolatry and deviation from Scripture, and the other liberal, which attacked Catholic dogmatism and superstition.[29] The latter form is now far more prevalent than the former, and many of its chief proponents might best be classed as 'Protestant atheists'. This is in some degree a sign of the continuing role of religious denominations in influencing the outlook even of those who seem to have left them far behind.

There are also a number of areas where religion once had a conspicuous role, but this has become increasingly less visible as these areas have become the preserve of professionals, who jealously guard their territory against intruders, their key weapon being the development of an arcane language incomprehensible to everyone else. The supersession of religious language by scientific or professional language has been seen in many spheres. It began in the natural sciences back in the mid-Victorian period, when the anti-religious passion of such scientists as T. H. Huxley derived from the conviction that science had to establish its autonomy. In the early Victorian period, many scientists were clergymen or devout laymen, who believed that studying nature meant studying the works of God, and that observation of nature would provide evidence in support of the most popular of the theistic proofs, namely the argument from design. But what if the Christian scientist were to discover evidence that weakened this argument? Huxley held that it was vital for scientific progress that no such conflict of loyalties should exist: scientists must be, above all, professionals, who would pursue a line of enquiry regardless of its consequences, and whose research was not influenced by assumptions about any supernatural power, lying beyond the boundaries of scientific proof. Huxley won this battle, and he would no doubt have seen it as a victory for the untrammelled pursuit of truth. A more cynical way of describing what happened would be to see it as the emergence of a new profession with a vested interest in the supremacy of some particular kinds of explanation and the exclusion of others.[30]

We can see similar processes in the rise of the medical and social work professions. For instance, the nineteenth century saw the decline of theological explanations of epidemics and the rise of medical explanations. The cholera epidemic of 1831–32 was widely seen as a divine visitation, and a Day of Fasting and Humiliation was prescribed by the Government. The epidemic ended soon afterwards, and many people saw this as an answer to prayer. Yet, within a very short time, the medical interpretation was superseding theological approaches, even within religious circles. The 1848–49 epidemic was, indeed, accompanied by a temporary religious revival, as sinners flocked into the churches to pray for escape, or maybe to put themselves right with God before it was too late. But this time there was no national day of prayer, and the Bishop of London, in speaking about the epidemic in the House of Lords, put the main stress on the need for more effective public health measures. In 1854, at the time of yet another cholera epidemic, Lord Palmerston rejected calls for a national day of prayer, arguing that prayers were only appropriate after all possible medical and sanitary precautions had been taken. (It should, however, be noted that when, in the same year, the Crimean War broke out, the Government did order a national day of prayer: which illustrates again the point that rather than there being a uniform decline in the use of religious language, such language has continued to flourish in some areas of life, while seeming increasingly out of place in others.)[31]

Some of the complexities of the situation are indicated by the example of changes in the stated rationale and methods of working of charitable organizations. Victorian England was awash with Christian charities. They often announced their Christianity in their title, their agents tended to be fervent Christians who felt they had a duty to proclaim their beliefs to anyone who was willing to listen, and many of those who would have preferred not to, and their work characteristically combined caring with evangelism. They would no doubt have argued that caring for the whole person included paying attention to their spiritual, as well as their physical, needs. And they were certainly aware that the material need suffered by large sections of the population provided evangelists with a golden opportunity for preaching the gospel while responding to these needs. As one typical example I would mention the London-based Ranyard Mission, founded in 1857, which employed nurses who would visit the sick in their homes, combining free medical care with a religious message.[32]

Certainly, there are many charities today which have an explicitly Christian rationale, and which mix charity with evangelism. However, the prevailing tendency is for organizations which have a Christian inspiration to play this fact down. For instance, in recent years the Church of England Children's Society has become simply the Children's Society. The chief reason for this seems to be the fear that those who are in need, but who are not Christians, may be frightened off if any explicit religious message is delivered. A good example of this situation would be the Samaritans, founded in 1953 to provide sympathetic listeners to whom those contemplating suicide could talk. The organization was founded by a London vicar, the Revd Chad Varah, and many of those working for the organization have been Christians. But in responding to the distress of those who telephone the organization, volunteers are prohibited from proposing a religious solution or, indeed, from raising the subject of religion at all, unless it has first been introduced by the person at the other end of the line.[33] This example seems to be characteristic in several ways. There are strong reasons for arguing that in a pluralistic society a charity will fulfil its stated objectives more effectively if it is religiously neutral. Yet it remains the fact that a high proportion of charitable initiatives have a mainly religious inspiration. Research by Robin Gill also suggests that active church-members have a level of involvement in voluntary organizations that is far above the national average.[34] So we have a situation where the link between religion and charity remains vitally important, but it has become partly hidden because of the exigencies of working in a pluralist society.

The role of religion in politics offers some parallels. Certainly, the political importance of issues relating to the church has greatly declined since the Victorian period, or even since the early years of this century. In spite of the temporary interest aroused by the debate over the ordination of women, no church issue in recent years has aroused the passion that surrounded the parliamentary debate over the Revised Prayer Book in 1927.[35] One could also draw a contrast between the rhetoric of Winston Churchill, on the one hand, and of Margaret Thatcher and John Smith on the other. Churchill, who was not a professing Christian, nonetheless used a Christian rhetoric, which he presumably regarded as meaningful to the majority of the British people, when defending 'Christian civilization' against the Nazi barbarians.[36] Thatcher and Smith both spoke as professing Christians and used Christian language when addressing such audiences as the General Assembly of the Church of Scotland (in Thatcher's case) or (in Smith's case) the readers of a collection of essays by Labour MPs advocating Christian Socialism.[37] But in addressing the House of Commons or the general public both used a religiously neutral language. So Christians are still politically significant as a relatively numerous section of public opinion, whose support politicians would like, and as an important influence on the thinking of many individuals prominent in public life. But one could well argue that religion has no direct part in public debate.

The effects of this growing pluralism have also been reflected in changes in the law. One could point, for instance, to the far-reaching changes since the 1960s in the law relating to questions of sexual morality. In a variety of areas, laws which were justified as an expression of Christian moral principles have been replaced by others founded on the recognition of current moral pluralism, and usually taking the form of a compromise between the demands of the various concerned lobbies. Major landmarks include the liberalizing Obscene Publications Act of 1959, followed by the publication in 1960 of *Lady Chatterley's Lover*, the legalization of homosexual acts between consenting adults in private in 1967, and, in the same year, a drastic extension of the circumstances in which abortions were legally permitted, and the Divorce Law Reform Act of 1969.[38] It must be stressed that these changes do not reflect any straightforward passage from a Christian to a secularist basis for our laws. Certainly, in every case there were Christians on both sides of the argument, and though most secularists probably supported these changes, one cannot speak of any unified secular lobby.

To illustrate these points, I shall indulge for a moment in a reminiscence from the 1960s, when I was a student at Cambridge, and was invited by a friend to join him at a meeting of the Cambridge Humanists, which was to be addressed by the Bishop of Woolwich, John Robinson, then something of a celebrity because of his best-selling work of popular theology, *Honest to God*. The chairman introduced the bishop by saying that Humanists fell into two groups – what he called the 'SCM type of Humanist', who believed in inter-faith dialogue, and the 'CICCU type' who cherished the slogan 'Death to the infidel'.[39] He belonged to the SCM type, and so welcomed the opportunity of listening to the other side. In similar spirit, the bishop delivered an exceedingly eirenic speech, in which he emphasized everything that Christians and Humanists had in common, and played down everything that divided them. However, in one corner of the room there was a group who evidently belonged to the 'CICCU type', and who were getting increasingly impatient with this atmosphere of tolerance and brotherly love. In the end, one of them shouted out: 'You've been telling us about all the things that Christians and Humanists can agree upon, like fighting world hunger and homelessness. But what about abortion? You would never find a Christian and a Humanist agreeing about that!' To which the bishop replied in his mild-mannered way 'Well, I do happen to be a Vice-President of the Abortion Law Reform Association'.[40]

So the claim sometimes heard, that laws founded on Christianity have given way to laws founded on secular Humanism, is triply misleading. In the first place, as I briefly suggested in the earlier part of this chapter, it is a drastic oversimplification to suppose that our laws, as they existed in the Victorian period, or in the first half of this century, were 'founded on Christianity' – though Christians certainly had more influence on their framing than they do now. In the second place, there is no consensus, either among Christians or among Humanists, over most of the debated issues. And in the third place, most of these controversies have been resolved, at least for the time being, by finding a compromise which is unacceptable to the more militant pressure-groups, but is acceptable to public opinion, which is generally more confused – partly because it recognizes the force of some of the arguments on each side. Equally questionable is the view that a rational and utilitarian basis for our laws has come to replace a moral or religious one.[41] In most of these areas of controversy, the competing lobbies are motivated by passionately held religious or moral principles, and while none of these lobbies is usually strong enough to impose its own viewpoint, each makes its essential contribution to the process of negotiation by which the final compromise is reached.[42] The 1967 Abortion Act, and subsequent modifications to the Act, provide a characteristic example. The main antagonists in the debate have been Catholics, believing, on the grounds of religious principle, in the child's absolute right to life, and feminists, maintaining, on equally principled grounds, the mother's absolute right to choose. The resulting laws provide for legal abortion, but only under certain conditions, and so are unsatisfactory to both parties. But the need for a compromise reflected the fact that both parties were strong enough to have to be taken into account in the determination of the final outcome.

There remain some areas of life in which the predominance of religious language and rites remains largely unchallenged. The most notable example would be the prevalence of Christian funerals. The British Humanist Association has devised alternative rites, and some inventive individuals have worked out their own ways of remembering their loved ones. But as yet these are very much minority options. Returning to my earlier model of two small but well-organized camps fighting for influence over a large uncommitted group: one could say that these alternative rites are largely the preserve of the convinced unbelievers, and that the uncommitted overwhelmingly choose to make use of Christian rites.

A second example is that of the attempts by the Christian churches to act as some kind of national conscience, or the demand that they should act in this way. The potential importance of the church, even in a relatively secularized society, as a focus for popular discontent and, in particular, as a critic of the morality of government policies, was demonstrated in a number of countries in the 1980s.[43] Admittedly, many of them had governments that were totalitarian, as in East Germany, or at least highly authoritarian, as in South Africa and Brazil. In more democratic and pluralist societies the voice of the churches is likely to be less important, simply because so many other forms of protest are available. But in Britain, too, the policies pursued by the Government in the 1980s were subject to considerable criticism by the churches. Indeed, the Thatcher Government received more religiously-based criticism than any other British administration of this century. The apparent toleration by the Government of levels of unemployment unknown since the 1930s, the shifting of the tax burden away from the rich and onto the shoulders of the poor, the less favourable treatment by the Government of pensioners and those on social security, and the more confrontational style of leadership adopted by Thatcher and her Ministers, were seen by many people to raise moral issues, which demanded more than a purely political critique. There were many moral critiques of Thatcherism. But it was those emanating from the churches, and especially those from the two national churches, which received most public attention. The reason for this seems to be that the churches are still seen as uniquely qualified to make moral judgements, uncontaminated by political partisanship, and, indeed, that many people would have felt that the churches were failing in their duty if they had not attempted to respond to these Government policies.[44]

It is a tribute to the effectiveness of these criticisms that Margaret Thatcher felt obliged to hit back by asserting the theological rationale for her policies in the famous 'Sermon on the Mound', addressed to the General Assembly of the Church of Scotland. This, as I see it, arose from a recognition that, though Thatcherism had made a successful appeal to the pockets of an important section of the electorate, it had been less successful in winning hearts and minds. Challenging her religious critics, by demonstrating Thatcherism's claim to be a legitimate expression of Christianity, was seen as a significant step towards the achievement of this objective.

The religious changes described in this chapter might be likened to the situation in a country with many local languages, one of which has for long enjoyed the status of a lingua franca, but where the inhabitants of another powerful region resent this primacy and are refusing to use the common language: as a result, it is gradually slipping back to the status of a purely local language. This, however, has led to a very confused situation whenever natives of the various regions meet together for trade or politics, or when they want to socialize together. In some areas of life, Esperanto has been introduced. It offends nobody, but it does not move or excite anybody either, and it can only express a narrow range of emotions. In other areas, the atmosphere is more like that of an international conference in which everyone is allowed to use their own language, and participants attend a few sessions where the language is one they understand, and ignore the rest. Some occupational groups, drawn from different regions, have devised their own professional language, which serves their own purposes well, but cannot be transferred to other contexts. In a neighbouring country, faced with similar problems, a revolutionary government has tried to impose a new lingua franca, but with disastrous results – the majority of people refused to use it, and many said they preferred the old language. So in the end an impasse has been reached.

Large parts of the old lingua franca have dropped out of general use, but no more acceptable alternative vocabularies have been found. In some areas of life the result is simply a void. In others, the lack of any convincing alternatives means that most people cling to the old words.

Notes

1. Joseph Butler, *The Analogy of Religion* (1736), Advertisement.
2. Victor Kiernan, 'Evangelicalism and the French Revolution', *Past & Present* 1 (1952), pp. 44–56.
3. W. R. Ward, *Religion and Society in England 1790–1850* (London, 1972); A. D. Gilbert, *Religion and Society in Industrial England 1740–1914: Church, Chapel and Social Change* (London, 1976); Deryck Lovegrove, *Established Church, Sectarian People* (London, 1988).
4. A comprehensive synthesis of recent work is provided by Gerald Parsons (ed.), *Religion in Victorian Britain* (4 vols, Manchester, 1988).
5. For organized secularism, see Edward Royle, *Radicals, Secularists and Republicans: Popular Freethought in Britain 1866–1915* (Manchester, 1980); for church membership statistics, Robert Currie, Alan Gilbert and Lee Horsley, *Churches and Churchgoers: Patterns of Church Growth in the British Isles Since 1700* (Oxford, 1977); for church attendance statistics, Robin Gill, *The Myth of the Empty Church* (London, 1993).
6. See, for instance, Parsons, op. cit., 2, pp. 166–298; Richard J. Helmstadter and Bernard Lightman (eds), *Victorian Faith in Crisis* (London, 1990); E. R. Wickham, *Church and People in an Industrial City* (London, 1957); Hugh McLeod, *Class and Religion in the Late Victorian City* (London, 1974), ch. 8; Jeffrey Cox, *English Churches in a Secular Society: Lambeth 1870–1930* (Oxford, 1982), chs 7–8.
7. Paul Badham (ed.), *Religion, State and Society in Modern Britain* (Lewiston, 1989), provides a comprehensive overview of contemporary religious trends. Peter Brierley, *Prospects for the Nineties* (London, 1991), provides useful statistics of Christian church adherence and attendance.
8. Cox, op. cit., ch. 4 provides a good account of the extent, and some of the limitations, of this taken-for-granted Christianity in late Victorian and Edwardian London.
9. Ibid, pp. 95–7. Thomas W. Laqueur's important study, *Religion and Respectability: Sunday Schools and Working Class Culture 1780–1850* (New Haven, 1976), is mainly concerned with the early nineteeth century.
10. Hugh McLeod, *Religion and the Working Class in Nineteenth-Century Britain* (Basingstoke, 1984), pp. 36–43.
11. See Sarah Williams, 'Religious belief and popular culture: a study of the South London Borough of Southwark, c. 1880–1939' (DPhil thesis, University of Oxford, 1993).
12. Catherine Moriarty, 'Christian iconography and First World War memorials', *Imperial War Museum Review* 6 (1992), pp. 63–75; Bob Bushaway, 'Name upon name: remembrance and the First World War' in Roy Porter (ed.), *Myths of the English* (London, 1992), pp. 136–67; Alan Borg, *War Memorials from Antiquity to the Present* (London, 1991).
13. Alan Wilkinson, *The Church of England and the First World War* (London, 1978), pp. 156–8; D. S. Cairns (ed.), *The Army and Religion* (London, 1919), p. 172.
14. Robert Tressell, *The Ragged Trousered Philanthropists* (London, 1955 [first published 1914]), p. 153.
15. Owen Chadwick, *The Victorian Church* (2 vols, London, 1966–70), 2, pp. 186–96, 299–308.

16. Hugh McLeod, 'White collar values and the role of religion' in Geoffrey Crossick (ed.), *The Lower Middle Class in Britain 1870–1914* (London, 1977), p. 80.
17. For the role of religion in the Victorian public school, see David Newsome, *Godliness and Good Learning* (London, 1961).
18. Chadwick, op. cit., 2, pp. 439–62; V. H. H. Green, *Religion at Oxford and Cambridge* (London, 1964), p. 339.
19. Keith Thomas, 'The double standard', *Journal of the History of Ideas* 20 (1959), pp. 195–216.
20. Lilian Lewis Shiman, *Women and Leadership in Nineteenth-Century England* (Basingstoke, 1992), pp. 138–50; Alison Milbank, 'Josephine Butler: Christianity, feminism and social action' in Jim Obelkevich, Lyndal Roper and Raphael Samuel (eds), *Disciplines of Faith* (London, 1987), pp. 154–64.
21. Carl Chinn, *Better Betting with a Decent Feller* (Brighton, 1991).
22. See, for instance, Stephen Koss, *Nonconformity in Modern British Politics* (London, 1975), p. 184, noting that by the 1930s all three major parties included significant numbers of Nonconformists. Peter G. Richards, *Parliament and Conscience* (London, 1970), p. 199, argued that since both main parties attracted supporters from a mixture of different religious groups, British governments tended to avoid issues that raised religious or moral issues, for fear of alienating some of their own voters.
23. Gill, op. cit., p. 301.
24. Williams, op. cit., pp. 231–54; Elizabeth Roberts, *Working Class Barrow and Lancaster, 1890 to 1930* (Lancaster, 1976), pp. 62–4.
25. For the decline in baptisms, see Gill, op. cit., p. 218. For some discussion of reasons why non-church-going parents want to have their babies christened, see Grace Davie and Geoffrey Ahearn, *Inner City God* (London, 1989).
26. George Moyser, 'In Caesar's service? Religion and political involvement in Britain' in Badham (ed.), op. cit., p. 354.
27. D. Butler and D. Stokes, *Political Change in Modern Britain* (London, 1974), pp. 156–7, report the case of one respondent who first of all said he had no religion and was asked by the interviewer whether he was atheist or agnostic, but, after an explanation of what these terms meant, said 'I think you'd better put me down as Church of England'.
28. The leading authority on contemporary English Catholicism, Michael Hornsby-Smith, stresses the decline of the Catholic subculture since the time of Vatican II and, indeed, argues that even before that time the extent of Catholic difference has been exaggerated. See, for instance, his *Roman Catholics in England* (Cambridge, 1987). Nonetheless, there are still many areas of Catholic belief and practice which are either unique to them or very unusual among non-Catholics – e.g. loyalty to the Pope, devotion to Mary and other saints, interest in shrines such as Lourdes. Even more distinctive is the intensity of the relationships, whether positive or negative, between lay Catholics and priests or nuns. And the most significant pointer to the continuing differences between Catholic and Protestant identity is the frequency with which ex-Catholics engage in an obsessive denigration of their former church, which is seldom emulated by those who have left other churches.
29. Graham Walker and Tom Gallagher (eds), *Sermons and Battle Hymns: Protestant Popular Culture in Modern Scotland* (Edinburgh, 1990) provides extensive discussion of anti-Catholicism in modern Scotland. In England such prejudice is less organized (the Orange Order is a highly localized phenomenon) and less visible (there is no equivalent of Glasgow Rangers), but it is nonetheless widespread.
30. Frank M. Turner, 'The Victorian conflict between science and religion: a professional dimension' in Parsons (ed.), op. cit., 4, pp. 170–97.
31. R. J. Morris, *Cholera 1832* (London, 1976).

32. Frank Prochaska, 'Body and soul: Bible nurses and the poor in Victorian London', *Historical Research* 60 (1987), pp. 336–48.
33. Chad Varah (ed.), *The Samaritans* (London, 1965), pp. 42–5.
34. Gill, op. cit., p. 204.
35. See Adrian Hastings, *A History of English Christianity 1920–1985* (London, 1986), pp. 203–8.
36. Keith Robbins, *History, Religion and Identity in Modern Britain* (London, 1993), p. 195.
37. Jonathan Raban, *God, Man and Mrs Thatcher* (London, 1989); Christopher Bryant (ed.), *Reclaiming the Ground: Christianity and Socialism* (London, 1993).
38. See Ian Machin, 'British churches and moral change in the 1960s' in W. M. Jacob and Nigel Yates (eds), *Crown and Mitre: Religion and Society in Northern Europe Since the Reformation* (Woodbridge, 1993), pp. 223–41.
39. The Student Christian Movement (SCM) and the Cambridge Inter-Collegiate Christian Union (CICCU) were the two main religious groups in the university, the former being liberal and ecumenical, and the latter being conservative and strictly confined to evangelical Protestants.
40. Robinson had given evidence for the defence at the Lady Chatterley trial, for which he was rebuked by the then Archbishop of Canterbury, Geoffrey Fisher. See Machin, op. cit., pp. 228–31, who stresses the divisions among Christians on this and related issues.
41. Christie Davies, *Permissive Britain: Social Change in the Sixties and Seventies* (London, 1975), argues for the prevalence among the law-makers of this period of a kind of utilitarianism that he terms 'causalist'. For instance, he compares (p. 39) the parliamentary debates on the abolition of capital punishment in 1948 and 1964, concluding that moralistic arguments predominated on the former occasion and pragmatic arguments on the latter occasion.
42. And indeed there is a sizeable minority of MPs whose voting on certain issues seems to be strongly influenced by their own religious or moral convictions. Richards, op. cit., pp. 182–4, analyses the relationship between the religious affiliations of MPs and their voting on a series of major social reforms in the 1960s. In some instances strong correlations were apparent. For instance, Nonconformists, Catholics, Jews and atheists/agnostics were far more likely than Anglicans or those of unknown religious affiliation to oppose capital punishment; Roman Catholics were far more likely than any other category of MP to oppose liberalization of the laws on abortion and divorce; and Nonconformists were most likely to oppose reform of the laws on Sunday entertainment. Atheists/agnostics were by far the most likely to support divorce law reform.
43. John Sandford, *The Sword and and the Ploughshare: Autonomous Peace Initiatives in East Germany* (London, 1983); John De Gruchy, *The Church Struggle in South Africa* (2nd edn, London, 1986); Scott Mainwaring, *The Catholic Church and Politics in Brazil 1916–1985* (Stanford, 1986).
44. Henry Clark, *The Church Under Thatcher* (London, 1993); Hugo Young, *One of Us: A Biography of Margaret Thatcher* (revised edn, London, 1993), pp. 416–26; Mark Dorsett, 'Populistischer Konservatismus und elitärer Liberalismus? Margaret Thatcher und die Führungskräfte der "Church of England" 1979 bis 1990' in Martin Greschat and Jochen-Christoph Kaiser (eds), *Christentum und Demokratie im 20. Jahrhundert* (Stuttgart, 1992), pp. 134–49.

2
Can one speak of God or to God in education?

John M. Hull

In a word one can speak of God but one cannot speak to God, especially on behalf of others. In the classroom one speaks of God; in collective worship the claim is that one speaks to God. The first situation is legitimate but the second is not. It is sometimes said that in theology God can only be addressed: God is the eternal Thou. God cannot be spoken about. In education the opposite is the case. God cannot be addressed but can be spoken of.

Speaking to God in collective worship 1944–88

The 1944 Education Act required all pupils in county maintained schools to attend and take part in a daily act of collective worship unless withdrawn by their parents. The withdrawal clause was a unique feature of the provisions for religious education, and it applied both to the classroom teaching and to the collective worship. Thus we see that to some extent the right not to worship was acknowledged. 'To some extent', because the right lay with the parents, not with the pupils. The pupils could be withdrawn, but they could not on their own initiative withdraw. Moreover, the fact that withdrawal could be exercised by parents both from collective worship and from classroom religious education suggests that the difference between speaking of God and speaking to God was not recognized. It is also significant that the legislation did not attempt any definition of worship, apart from the adjective 'collective'. Worship was not to be of a denominational character. It was not to be characterized by the use of any catechism or formulary distinctive of a denomination, and was thus presumed to be rather general in nature. Nothing was said in

1944 about the purpose of collective worship. The theological element was thus minimized. The law did not even speak of collective worship as being Christian worship.

Thus it was that over the years a variety of interpretations and practices developed. On the one hand, there were school prayers. These generally took the form of a brief ceremony, perhaps of ten minutes' duration, in which there would be a hymn, a reading from the Bible and a prayer. Collective worship, or religious observances as they were previously called, was a simple service of worship addressed to God.

The other tradition took a broader and more imaginative view of the purpose and content of collective worship. Collective worship was more participatory, it often sprang out of work done in the classroom, particularly in primary schools. It involved the use of drama and dance, of debates and of reflections upon current affairs. A whole literature grew up giving examples of such collective worship, and the various magazines and journals used by teachers, especially RE teachers, almost always had a section devoted to what was variously called worship workshop, school assembly file, themes for worship and so on. This type of collective worship was often simply known as school assembly, and was regarded as being worshipful in the sense that the values and commitments of school life, and indeed of the community, were explored, affirmed and celebrated, but within a context of diversity rather than unanimity.

I shall refer to the more liturgical tradition as being the narrow or more explicitly theological understanding of collective worship, while the more general approach I will regard as representing a broader understanding of worship. Perhaps we might say that the narrow interpretation focused upon the object of worship, while the broader interpretation focused upon the reality of school life as being a collectivity, i.e. young people and adults gathered together from a variety of religious and, indeed, non-religious backgrounds and persuasions in a broadly worshipful manner. Needless to say, collective worship, whether of the narrow or the broad kind, was sometimes done well and sometimes done poorly or not at all.

The 1988 Education Reform Act

In 1988 the situation changed. The old legislation was carried forward and became Section 6 of the Education Reform Act. A new section was added, Section 7, in which an effort was made to offer a more precise theological definition of the nature and object of collective worship. Collective worship was to be 'wholly or mainly of a broadly Christian character', and the acts of collective worship were regarded as being wholly or mainly of a broadly Christian character if they reflected the 'broad traditions of Christian belief'. They were, however, not to be denominational in character. Moreover, not all of the acts of collective worship offered by a school need be of this character. It would be sufficient if in a given school term the majority of the acts of collective worship were wholly or mainly of a broadly Christian character. The other acts of collective worship, the minority of such acts, would not fall under Section 7, but under Section 6, the old 1944 section where collective worship was not defined. In considering the ways in which and the extent to which the daily acts of collective worship should fall under the requirement of Section 7, i.e. should be wholly or mainly of a broadly Christian character, headteachers were to take account of the ages, aptitudes and family backgrounds of their pupils. In all cases, however, the parental right of withdrawal was retained.

It took the schools some time to work out the implications of all this. LEAs produced guidelines,[1] RE advisers, inspectors and lecturers produced booklets interpreting the legislation and offering examples of the various types of assembly which could now be arranged,[2] and other bodies issued reports and guidelines.[3] It became clear that a school could offer an act of collective worship every day of the week which would be wholly of a broadly Christian character. On the other hand, it was also clear that no school was required ever to have an act of collective worship which was wholly of a broadly Christian character, because the law says 'wholly or mainly' of a broadly Christian character. What would collective worship be if it were only 'mainly of a broadly Christian character'? It quickly became apparent that acts of collective worship could be drawn from more than one religious tradition, and that what came to be called multi-faith worship was permitted by the law every day of the week, provided that on the whole on each day or on a majority of days the mainly Christian character could be demonstrated. Then there were the other days, when Section 6 collective worship could take place. Nothing was said in the law about the content or approach of such acts of collective worship; and thus we could assume that there was no reason why they should not be wholly or mainly of a broadly Muslim or Hindu character, depending upon the character of the school population. Headteachers were advised to keep records in case of disputes or complaints.

However, the keeping of records was no easy business. In order to be demonstrably of a 'wholly or mainly broadly Christian character', an act of collective worship was required to reflect the 'broad traditions of Christian belief'. This expression was unqualified and clearly somewhat ambiguous. The traditions to be followed are not those of Christian worship, since these were presumably almost always denominational and this is expressly forbidden, but would reflect the broad traditions of Christian belief. The traditions are multiple – it is the 'traditions' of Christian belief, not the 'tradition'; and one notes the word 'tradition' rather than the 'doctrines'. Traditions of belief rather than beliefs are what is in mind.

Moreover, the 'traditions' are not the specific traditions or the explicit traditions, but the 'broad traditions'. When you have satisfied yourself what the 'broad traditions of Christian belief' might be, you then have to take on board the fact that collective worship has to reflect these. It does not have to contain them or be based upon them, whatever these activities might be, but merely to reflect them.

Interpretations ranged again from the broad to the narrow. The narrow interpretation insisted that collective worship should be quite explicitly based on worship of the Holy Trinity and the doctrines of the early church councils. The broad definition suggested that love was characteristic of Christian belief and that if acts of collective worship expressed love of one's neighbour then at least one broad tradition of Christian belief was being reflected.

This complexity illustrates the problems which you run into when you try to speak to God in education. Which God are you speaking to? Are there fixed boundaries between the various religious traditions, the ones we call Christian, Muslim and so on, or are the boundaries rather flexible and porous? How are disputes in these areas to be decided, and by whom? What happens to the spirit of mutuality and celebration when one has to begin counting and measuring the degree to which one religion is mainly or wholly reflected, while others are reflected on a minority of days or in a minor way in an individual act of collective worship, or not at all? Is it good or bad for the personal and religious identity of children and young people that it should be done in one way or another?

Speaking to various Gods

You may think this is complicated, but we have only just started. It was clear in 1988 that even when qualified in the various ways described, collective worship which was wholly or even only mainly of a broadly Christian character would not be appropriate for all schools or for all pupils within those schools. Would there be massive withdrawals? If there were, would it matter? It would certainly be embarrassing if substantial numbers of pupils from Jewish, Hindu, Muslim, Sikh and other religious traditions were withdrawn, because that would suggest that the provisions of the school for the moral and spiritual development of its pupils were extended to one community but denied to others. A middle way had to be found between simple withdrawal and, on the other hand, general participation in the broadly Christian norm which the law envisaged.

An answer was found in the determination procedure. If a headteacher came to believe that the provisions of Section 7, however qualified and adapted, were still inappropriate for some or all of the pupils in the school, an application could be made to the local SACRE, the Standing Advisory Council on Religious Education, for the requirements of Section 7 to be lifted. When that happened, the SACRE was described as offering a determination to the school. A school could apply for a determination on behalf of any group of its pupils; more than one determination could be applied for.

Moreover, it was recommended that the school should look with sympathy upon the voluntary provision of acts of worship for those pupils who were withdrawn by their parents, whether from the Section 6 worship or the Section 7 worship or, indeed, from the determinated acts of collective worship, since the parental right of withdrawal remained absolute in all circumstances.

The schools thus found themselves in a situation of embarrassing richness. There could be acts of collective worship which were wholly Christian, others which were only mainly Christian, and these could take place on all or only most of the school days. The other acts of collective worship were unspecified and could be anything worshipful. In addition to this, there could be acts of collective worship which were determinated; and finally there could be acts of worship still supervised by the school staff but run by volunteers for pupils who were withdrawn by their parents because the latter were not satisfied with any of the abundant variety available. The whole thing was becoming an administrative and indeed a spiritual nightmare.

The rise of a theology of collective worship

Sandal Magna First School in Wakefield, Acton High School in London and Crowcroft Park Primary School in Manchester were all subjects of complaint from groups of parents, always of a very conservative outlook, who protested that their children were not receiving Christian worship; or were only receiving it sometimes; or were receiving it mixed up in a sort of hotchpotch with elements from other religions resulting in a confused mishmash.[4] The complaints all failed, and the flexibility and ambiguity of the law became even more obvious. The struggle to persuade the schools to speak to the Christian God seemed to be running into difficulties. To some extent the problem lay in the lack of definitions. The legal branch was advising the Government that without definitions there could not be successful proceedings in court.

Moreover, there had been disappointingly few determinations granted. As long as children from different faiths were worshipping together, there could be no purely and wholly Christian character. The Christian character of collective worship could not emerge clearly from a diverse school population. Diversity must be reduced in order to enable Christian unanimity to emerge uncompromised.

The determination procedure, at first merely looked upon as a safety valve or as a way of securing apparent equality for the various religions, now began to take on greater significance. This could be a way of purifying collective worship, of purifying through separating. But first, it would be necessary to make the theological profile of collective worship so sharp that separation would become inevitable.

At this point we reach the new Circular 1/94 issued by the Department for Education on 31 January 1994. Paragraph 50 deals with the aims of collective worship. These are

> to provide the opportunity for pupils to worship God, to consider spiritual and moral issues and to explore their own beliefs; to encourage participation and response, whether through active involvement in the presentation of worship or through listening to and joining in the worship offered; and to develop community spirit, promote a common ethos and shared values and reinforce positive attitudes.

Here we see what I have called the narrow and broad strands of interpretation coming together. The broad strand is affirmed through the attempt to promote a common ethos and shared values through participation of an exploratory kind. The more strictly theological interpretation lies in the opening definition: that pupils should be provided with an opportunity to worship God. For the first time in the history of school worship, the object of worship is stated. It is God. This was clearly written by a government which believes that it is not only possible but desirable, indeed mandatory, to speak to God in education. But who or what is God, and when would one know that God was being worshipped?

Paragraph 57 of the Circular turns to the question of 'the meaning of collective worship'. Now we read

> worship is not defined in the legislation and in the absence of any such definition it should be taken to have its natural and ordinary meaning. That is, it must in some sense reflect something special or separate from ordinary school activities and it should be concerned with reverence or veneration paid to a divine being or power.

This takes the specific or explicit theological definition a step further. But how is the diversity of commitment and belief to be recognized? The Draft Circular continues

> However, worship in schools will necessarily be of a different character from worship amongst a group with beliefs in common. The legislation reflects this difference in referring to 'collective worship' rather than 'corporate worship'. (paragraph 57)

It is thus recognized that the school community does not have 'beliefs in common'. Now, only in the previous sentence we were told that the natural and ordinary meaning of worship is that 'reverence or veneration [is] paid to a divine being or power'. If the worshippers share this belief, a belief upon which the possibility of it being worshipped at all is founded, they could be regarded as offering corporate worship. But they do not have beliefs in common, possibly not even the belief in a divine being or power to whom reverence and veneration are to be paid. It is precisely for this reason that the legislation calls the acts of worship collective rather than corporate. In other words, we are dealing with a collectivity of people with various beliefs and outlooks, not with a body or corpus of believers.

The Circular gives and then the Circular takes away. They must have beliefs in common in order to be able to worship, but at the same time it is recognized that they do not have beliefs in common. The whole conception of collective worship as that worship offered by people who do not have beliefs in common is so far from the natural and ordinary meaning of the word 'worship' that it is hard to see how in the natural and ordinary meaning such an activity can be called worship at all. From the point of view of the broad tradition of collective worship, that would not matter, since emphasis upon the educational context and a range of diverse beliefs has always been central to that broad interpretation. The Department is trying to have it both ways. On the one hand, they insist upon a theological definition of worship which demands unanimity; on the other hand, they assert that they fully recognize that the people gathering together for worship do not have unanimity.

Let us take up the question of the natural and ordinary meaning of the word 'worship'. The natural and ordinary meaning of the word 'worship' surely includes the assumption that the worshippers are of a common mind and are gathered together in a place which for this purpose can be called a place of worship. This would normally be a temple or a church, a mosque or a synagogue. In taking this natural and ordinary meaning of the word, the Department completely fails to recognize the context of the activity within the state school. After all, if we are to impose upon schools the natural and ordinary meaning of the word 'worship' then the school itself will by the same natural and ordinary meaning become a place of worship, and children and young people will become theists, active committed believers in a supreme or divine being or power, simply by virtue of having their names placed upon the registration records of the school. State education thus requires a form of religious commitment. At the same time, the Circular insists that 'this country has a long tradition of religious freedom which should be preserved' (paragraph 9).

I have referred to school pupils or students as being committed to active theism merely by having their names inscribed upon the registration roles of the school. You may say 'surely that is a mere formality. Do we need to take it in such an active and positive sense? Surely the pupils are not expected to speak to God?' The Circular soon gives us the answer. Paragraph 59 says that 'taking part in collective worship implies more than simply passive attendance. It follows that an act of collective worship should be capable of eliciting a response from pupils.' But will not some pupils be sceptics, or agnostics or even straightforward atheists? Let us not forget that the legislation applied to all young people in schools, including those aged over 16. Having said that the act of worship should be such as to elicit a response from pupils, the Circular adds 'even though on a particular occasion some of the pupils may not feel able actively to identify with the act of worship' (paragraph 59). Can it be said that this expression takes the religious life or the irreligious life of students seriously? There is no recognition of the possibility of genuine and sustained disbelief in God. It is difficult to resist the view that this amounts to a gross intrusion into the privacy, the rights of conscience, and thus of the religious freedom, which includes the freedom to be irreligious, of young people.

Towards a theology of Christian collective worship

So far so good. We have seen the contradictions and complexities which are created when one insists that God is addressed in education. But all this takes place under the descriptions of Section 6 of the ordinary act of worship. We have not yet even begun the attempt to give closer definition to Section 7, the section which requires collective worship to be 'wholly or mainly of a broadly Christian character'. We come to this under the section of the Circular headed 'The Character of Collective Worship'. This is important, because up until now we have not encountered anything which would divide Christians from Muslims and Jews. We have only encountered that which would divide believers in God from others. We still have not got the purity of Christian worship. This is to be achieved by the further definition offered at the end of paragraph 63.

Acts of collective worship must 'contain some elements which relate specifically to the traditions of Christian belief and which accord a special status to Jesus Christ' (paragraph 63). We can now see that every headteacher needs to have a certain theological expertise. What are these elements which relate specifically to the traditions of Christian belief? How are these to be decided upon in the case of complaint? Would it not be more helpful if the Department issued a list of such elements for the guidance of headteachers? Such guidance would be particularly helpful in the case of the 'special status' to be accorded to Jesus Christ. Is it enough, one wonders, for Jesus to have the status of being a teacher or a prophet? Would that be regarded as being specifically related to Christian belief? Or should the special status accorded to Jesus Christ, Jesus as Messiah, Jesus as Saviour, reflect his status as the incarnate Word of God, the Eternal Logos, the second person of the Trinity, the Son of the Father, begotten not made, being of one substance with the Father, light from light, God from God? How special does a Christology have to be before an act of worship can be regarded as being wholly of a broadly Christian character for most of the time?

Again, we must consider how active the participation of pupils is to be. We are now told that 'pupils who do not come from Christian families should be able to join in the daily act of collective worship even though this would, in the main, reflect the broad traditions of Christian belief' (paragraph 65). The Departmental Circular does not distinguish between pupils who come from secular or humanist homes and those who come from homes committed to Islam, Judaism or one of the other religious traditions. One might suppose that they were from humanist homes or from secular homes, since one would expect pupils from other religious traditions to be catered for by the determination procedure. In any case, it is difficult to see how either category of pupils can really be expected to respond to such acts of specific Christian worship. This country, we are reminded, has a long tradition of religious freedom which should be preserved.

In the light of all this, we can see what happens to the determination procedure. You will remember that this is the device whereby pupils from religions other than Christianity are to be provided with acts of collective worship. Paragraph 68 says that the determination procedure is to be invoked where the normal type of Christian collective worship would be 'inappropriate'. Behind that innocent little word we find the intention to divide pupils along religious lines. The technique is clear enough: first you raise the profile of worship, confining it to theists. Then you raise the theological profile of

Christian worship, excluding those who are not Christians. You thus *make* it inappropriate for any but Christians to take part, claiming the majority of the population as being at least in principle Christian, hiving the rest off into separate acts of worship.

In order to illustrate the harmful effect which this legislation is having upon schools I will describe briefly a situation known to me in a primary school in one of our large cities. 70 per cent of the boys and girls in the school are Muslims. The remainder are Hindus and Sikhs, with a few children from Christian backgrounds, mostly African British traditions. The chair of the Governing Body is a distinguished Muslim and several of the governors are also Muslim. Recently two or three of these Muslims have raised with the Governing Body a question of conscience to which they are sensitive. Although they do not object to anything which the school is actually doing in collective worship, they point out that it is nevertheless regarded in law as worship which is 'wholly or mainly of a broadly Christian character'. This is a problem for them, since technically their children are taking part, actively participating in programmes of worship which the school, if challenged, would have to insist were appropriately to be regarded as wholly or mainly of a broadly Christian character. It is not the actual practice of the school to which these Muslims object. If it were the case that their young people were being invited to pray to God the Holy Trinity or to offer prayer through Jesus Christ, this would clearly be objectionable. It is the official or legal status of what is going on that worries them. Now, the obvious solution would be for the school to seek a determination for those Muslim pupils. That would enable them to have worship which was wholly or mainly of a broadly Muslim character. The school is against this, however, because it would be left with a minority of its pupils in the act of collective worship, and it must be assumed that the Sikh and Hindu parents would follow suit, and further requests for determinations would follow. The school would then be divided along religious lines. Since this is a school in a multi-ethnic and multi-religious area which has done a great deal of work in holding the various communities together, it would regard this as a retrograde step. But what can be said to the Muslims? It is easy for those in a position of cultural dominance to pooh-pooh these concerns and to say 'but it is only the letter of the law to which you object'.

At this point, there is an interesting variation. The school might make application to its local SACRE for a determination which would apply not to any particular group of pupils on the basis of their distinct religious family background but to the entire school, so as to make possible acts of collective worship which would draw upon all the religious traditions represented in the school. The entire school would move back from Section 7 collective worship to Section 6 collective worship. A number of SACREs have accepted this type of determination; others have been less than happy. The proposal would open the door for what is sometimes called multi-faith worship or inter-faith worship, whereas the whole tenor of Section 7 is that worship is to be conducted along separate lines, religion by religion. Brenda Watson points out that

> a major criticism of the legislation . . . is that it assumes that worship must come under the umbrella of one or other religious tradition – however broadly this is understood – that all worship must be either Christian or Jewish or Muslim, and so on. It is this 'package' aspect of worship which is the real bone of contention dividing people into separate camps.[5]

Once the principle of whole-school determinations was widely accepted, it is difficult to see that much would remain in practice of Section 7 collective worship. Let us imagine a primary school in which there are 600 children from Christian family backgrounds and two or three Muslim children. The same arguments apply in principle as in the situation where 70 per cent of the pupils are Muslim. Either the two or three Muslim children are to be placed in an invidious position in which they are formally regarded as Christian worshippers, or the Christian children are to lose their right (as some would see it) to a distinctive act of Christian worship. Either way, the school and its community are almost sure to be plunged into controversy. However, if a whole-school determination lifted the requirement for broadly Christian collective worship, the school could continue with its all-embracing practice, to which no one objects. As to the right of the pupils from Christian family backgrounds to an act of distinctively Christian worship, this right should be exercised in a Christian place of worship. The school itself should not be regarded as such a place, and when Christians insist upon that right being exercised on the premises of the county school, they are engaged in a policy which is not truly Christian in spirit; if the law appears to support such a divisive policy, we must conclude that the law is inappropriate.

Paragraph 71 of Circular 1/94 says that in any arrangements to be made 'for a determination in relation to the whole school . . . care should be taken to safeguard the interests of any parents of children for whom broadly Christian collective worship would be appropriate'. Why so? Because the assumption and indeed the requirement of the law is that the Christian God is to be addressed. The Christian God is to have normative status. It is expected that the majority of pupils will find this appropriate. It is only non-Christian minorities or majorities who are to be catered for under the determination procedure. The needs of the Christian majority or minority are to be catered for under the normal arrangements of Section 7 collective worship. We also note that the Secretary of State has the power to intervene in the determination procedures of a local SACRE, and to prevent or overthrow a determination decision which he feels to be inappropriate (paragraph 81). Given the general character of the current Government, there is little doubt that the Education Secretary would consider it inappropriate if the legal intention to establish a more or less pure and consistent Christian worship alongside (if necessary and appropriate) a more or less pure and consistent worship in accordance with the beliefs of other religions were overthrown or evaded by a widespread use of the determination procedure.

That the collective worship requirements envisage prayer not only to God but to the Christian God, the Muslim God, the Hindu God and so on separately is borne out by the Government interpretation of the content of the agreed syllabuses. The legislation quite simply and rather vaguely requires that any new agreed syllabuses 'shall reflect the fact that the religious traditions in Great Britain are in the main Christian whilst taking account of the teaching and practices of the other principal religions represented in Great Britain' (Education Reform Act 1988, s. 8.3). Instead of acknowledging that this process of reflecting and taking account of could be represented in a wide range of syllabuses, as has in fact been the case for many years, the Government insists upon a sharp separation between the first and second parts of the sentence, demanding that agreed syllabuses should follow this structure, thus creating a situation in which religious education is to consist of nothing but the study of religions one by one in separate compartments. This interpretation has the advantage, from the Government's point of view, of preventing any speech about God which might imply that God is not confined within a specific religious tradition. There is to be no treatment of the religions of the world as if they were embarked upon a common enterprise, or were part of a single spiritual vocation of humanity, or were a response to the one lord over all who is rich unto all who call upon him or her. The second advantage is that, once this separation is insisted upon, it is possible to argue that children will be confused if they are involved in speech about more than, let us say, two or three Gods, and thus the preponderance of Christianity can be ensured. Comparison and measurement become possible. A 'balanced' religious education curriculum can be required. It is as if God were confined to the cultural, spiritual and religious traditions of human beings such that God could only be addressed in Hebrew or Arabic or Punjabi. Every time he is spoken of, the language is to be noted and the time is to be measured.

We see, then, that the Government policy on God-talk is consistent. One can speak both about God and to God, but preferably, and if possible always, to the separate God of each religious tradition, and normally and mainly to the Christian God. My own view is that in religious education there can and should be speech about God both within each separate religious tradition and as being a reality beyond the limits of any one religious tradition or of all of them put together. God is great. God is that greater than which nothing can be conceived. 'Behold, heaven and the highest heaven cannot contain thee, how much less this house [religion, tradition, curriculum, act of worship] which I have built!' (1 Kings 8.27). Your God is too small.

On the other hand, one may not speak to God on behalf of others. Not only is this impudent; it is an affront to the spiritual rights of children. God may be addressed in collective worship, but only in the spirit of reciprocal witness. You may share your faith with me in the sense that you may witness to your faith. You may not assume that your faith is my faith. What we must seek in collective worship is not an inclusive hegemony nor an exclusive multiplicity, but an inclusive diversity. This demands a low theological definition and an acceptance of the broad tradition of collective worship. If that can be achieved, we will find that we dare speak of God in education, since all our speech, whether of God or to God, will be in God's presence.

Notes

1. Kent County Council, *Collective Worship: A Guide to Good Practice* (Maidstone: KCC, 1991); London Borough of Redbridge, *School Worship: Perspectives and Principles* (Redbridge, 1991).
2. Terence Copley, *Worship, Worries and Winners* (London: National Society, 1989); Bill Gent, *School Worship: Perspectives, Principles and Practice* (Derby: CEM, 1989).
3. British Council of Churches, *Worship in Education* (London, 1989); Secondary Heads Association, *Collective Worship* (Occasional Paper 89/2; SHA, 1989); *Multi-Faith Worship?* (London: Church House Publishing, 1992).
4. I have discussed the metaphors of mixed and often disgusting food which became common in the political rhetoric which surrounded RE and collective worship in my booklet *Mishmash: Religious Education in Multi-Cultural Britain: A Study in Metaphor* (Derby: CEM, 1991; ISBN 1-85100-043-7).
5. Brenda Watson, *The Effective Teaching of Religious Education* (London: Longman, 1993), pp. 161–2.

3
Can we speak of God in the secular academy? Or, need theology be so useless?

Stephen Pattison

Theology made me. More precisely, most of my early life from my teens to my mid-thirties has been shaped academically by the discipline of Christian theology and personally by active Christian commitment in the church. I cannot get away from it – I am a Christian theologian, one whose intellect and world-view is bounded and informed by long-standing critical engagement with Christian ideas and practices. And I am not just a generic theologian, i.e. one who thinks critically about how people think about God using philosophical, literary, sociological and other tools of the human sciences.. I am a practical theologian – one who tries to discern the practical implications of belief and thought for action and vice versa, and to construct action-guiding principles which have regard to ideas, principles and practices generated from within (if not solely from within) communities of religious commitment and belief. To be more specific still, I am a critical practical theologian of care; a person who seeks to analyse and create action-guiding strategies of religiously-informed care which will preserve, develop and enrich human well-being within a horizon of faith.

Theology may have made me, but it does not keep me. I work in a definitely secular context, writing open learning materials about health and social welfare for people of all faiths and none. In this context, I somewhat coyly describe myself as a wordsmith. But does this do justice to the reality of my past and my basic discipline? Can I take theology with me? Or, in a curious inversion of the story of Moses and the burning bush, must I discard it as I enter the university campus, for where I stand now is secular ground? In personal terms, this is a question of whether my training and past endeavours have any value for me now, whether I have any contribution to make, or whether my activity as a theologian has been some kind of mistake. In academic terms, this poses the question: 'Is theology, and practical theology in particular, of any use to anyone other than theologians and practising Christians?' Should I and others regard theology as useless or useful? I want to argue in this chapter that aspects of Christian theology should be more useful in secular contexts than they might presently be perceived to be.

I seek to address two audiences. The first, and main, audience is that of the colleagues I have left behind in theology who often seem firmly trapped in an obscurantist religious ghetto. I hope to challenge them to come out of the closet and share some of their skills and expertise in quarters where they may feel they have little to offer. The second audience is that of my new colleagues, some of whom feel vaguely embarrassed that they have a Christian theologian working with them and prefer to introduce me to people as an ethics or public service management specialist. I am neither: in terms of academic expertise I am a pastoral theologian. I need to explain what theology can offer to non-Christian non-theologians, so that my expertise can become an asset, not a liability or irrelevance, to me and to the organization in which I work. To put it in the helpful jargon of my institution, I have to articulate and demonstrate the competencies, skills and content which are transferable from directly theological activity into other academic pursuits oriented towards education and training aimed at producing human well-being and care.

Obstacles

There are considerable obstacles to commending and demonstrating the usefulness and importance of theological insights, methods and skills in the the contemporary world in general and in the academy in particular. Theology's close association with the practice of institutional Christian religion, the source of much of its life and such interest as it possesses, makes it deeply suspect for many.

Intellectually, Christianity, in common with other religions, is subject to the classic critiques of suspicion which hold that it is a dysfunctional projection (Freud), an ideological tool of social control (Marx), or an alienation of human potential (Nietzsche). Historically, the record of Christianity shows it as morally ambivalent at best, oppressive, violent and bigoted at worst. In the present, it is more or less socially tolerable as a repository of quaint archaism providing personal support for consenting adults in private (though still prone to unfortunate bouts of injustice and prejudice against groups whom others have come to accept, e.g. women and gays). In its virulent fundamentalist forms, however, it is rejected as nakedly authoritarian, dogmatic, intolerant and regressive. Those who have encountered Christianity in their childhood often regard their escape from it as emancipation. Small wonder, in the light of all this, that the advent of a theologian in a secular university department feels like returning to the dark ages of superstition and repression for many self-respecting liberal academics (even those who have personal religious commitments).

But theologians do not make it easy for others to appreciate what they have to offer either. Until very recently, if not now, we have bound ourselves closely (even organically) and quite narrowly to the institutions, practices and concerns of established Christian churches. (Many theologians have been clergy and the organization of theology at Oxbridge was heavily clerically dominated until very recently.) The by-products of this have been various and considerable.

First, despite protestations from some quarters that we have 'let the world write the agenda', we have allowed intra-religious preoccupations and concerns to dominate our thinking (the global crisis or the future of the welfare state, for example, are still low on the list of priorities for consideration in both church and academy). Christian theology is still largely confessional theology, taught mostly by believers to believers, addressing the concerns of believers.

Secondly, following the direction set by the earliest theologians of churches (the so-called 'Fathers'), we have been preoccupied with the cognitive aspects of belief. This means that when people talk of 'theology' they are alluding to the cognitive, dogmatic aspects of belief, not to non-cognitive matters such as basic trust, mythology, emotion or practice. (Hence, in part, the low status of practical, operation- or action-centred theology within the academy.)

Thirdly, because we have been concerned with matters of communal identity and legitimation, we have been largely engaged in looking backwards, exploring the tradition and ancient authoritative texts of this religion rather than with studying matters of contemporary general human concern.

To crown it all, and as a consequence of all these, we have chosen to explore our concerns in concepts and language which are complex, technical and obscure to non-initiates. The reviews editor for a national paper told me recently: 'I simply cannot recommend theological books for review because they appear to be written in a private language!'

A caricature of the academic discipline of contemporary theology would see it as cognitively and communally confined, privatized, jargonized, narrow, impractical, anachronistic, nostalgic and ecclesiocentric. And that is even before one takes on the major content difficulties of theology, such as the existence and nature of God, the nature of revelation etc., all of which are likely to be problematic in the sceptical contemporary academy. The image of David Lodge's fictional radical atheist Catholic theologian Bernard Walsh writing a book review on process theology which no one is likely to read for *Eschatological Review* is a telling and ironic icon here:

> It often seemed to Bernard that the discourse of much modern radical theology was just as implausible and unfounded as the orthodoxy it had displaced, but nobody had noticed because nobody read it except those with a professional stake in its continuation.[1]

There are many factors militating against the acceptance of this kind of academic theology into a wider academic world. If any theologian should doubt this, let him or her enquire of non-theologian colleagues when they last read a serious theological book and the reasons for their not doing so. The age of interdisciplinary enquiry has dawned with a vengeance. But consider the influence of thinkers like Foucault, Derrida or Habermas over many disciplines, compared to the influence of almost any major contemporary theologian you care to name. (Perhaps the last theologian to have a major influence outwith the world of church and theological faculty was the social theologian Reinhold Niebuhr.) Even those who bother to address the secular academy, like David Tracy, have few non-theological readers.[2] Theology is not even in the rearguard of knowledge. Many of its better ideas and methods are derived from other disciplines anyway. The waters appear to grow ever more stagnant in this backwater of academic life.

Perhaps, then, at this point I should opt out of the struggle to assert that theology can be useful outside a very narrow context. There are too many walls, too many difficulties. Maybe, like Moses, I should turn my back on Egypt and head for the promised land, taking nothing with me and hoping that soon neither I nor those around me will remember my dubious academic past. But this would be to lose and deny too much. I am a critical practical theologian of care. Are there not things that I can and should profitably take with me into my secular environment for my own good and that of those already there? I think there must be.

Theological offerings

The one thing you cannot leave behind when you travel is your self, as many unhappy would-be escapees know to their frustration. Whether I like it or not, my intellectual life and personality have been shaped by theology and engagement with Christianity, and this continues to have an impact on the way I see the world and my interactions with it. To be a theologian is to acquire habits of mind and practice, to become a certain kind of character with certain skills.

This may seem a banal and minimalistic assertion, but I think it is important. It is often assumed in theology conceived of as overt consideration of explicit dogma that only when one is using technical theological jargon is one doing theology or contributing a theologically-based viewpoint. If theology could come down off its cognitive perch, keep quiet and engage in common discussion using non-technical language, there would be more hope that it could contribute seriously to discussions of greater general significance than is the case at the moment. (Who wants to be preached at by a gaggle of verbose 'vicars' talking in a private polysyllabic code?) The effective and acceptable theological contribution in the secular environment will often depend on the sort of person one has become and one's implicit frame of reference, not on a showy pyrotechnical display of jargon (which might in any case be a substitute for thought and serious engagement as well as a cover for considerable insecurity!).

Emphasizing the character and intellectual habits of the theologian as a contribution to general discourse is not enough. It must be possible to be more explicit about what transferable skills, competencies and knowledge a theologian can offer. In a moment, I will go on to say more about this. However, two preliminary remarks must be made. First, I very much doubt whether the overt fideistic cognitive content of theological discourse can be of much use in dialogues in the secular academy. The content of belief really has become largely a private matter these days and people will not usually take kindly to overt evangelism. Theological concepts can have some place. Theological questions and methods can have a large place, particularly if they are not tagged as theologically derived. I will demonstrate the utility of this later.

Following on from this, I think it must be owned that it is most unlikely that theological distinctiveness lies in a monopoly of particular methods, insights or questions. Academic theology itself is composed of insights and methods from many other sources, e.g. literary criticism, hermeneutics, history, sociology, philosophy, anthropology. The distinctiveness of the theological contribution lies in the particular combination and configuration of these insights within certain definite horizons of concern and discourse. Theologians do not know better (though many behave as though they do). They simply know differently because of their particular training and life experience. It is this difference which needs to be articulated and offered appropriately and sensitively within the secular academy. So, what kind of usefulness might my particular experience and training as a practical theologian of care offer to the overall project of seeking general human health and social welfare, the enterprise which my job now requires me to pursue?[3]

One important but not particularly exalted contribution which can be made to the general quest for human health and social welfare is simply to provide information about the religious community, its history, practices, present state and preoccupations. In the understandable flight from religion as superstition, and Christianity as dominant religion, into the modern democratic state where no one should be prized or discriminated against for their colour, creed, sex or social status, it can easily be forgotten that many of our social assumptions and institutions have been formed partly by religious groups and views. Examples can be multiplied of social reformers and organizations whose activity was motivated at least in part by religious preoccupations (Shaftesbury, Tawney, Temple, Relate).[4] Having some kind of empathic understanding of how religion has interacted with social institutions may be a very important clue to the nature of these same institutions today.

Even more important is to have some understanding of how religion functions in people's lives today. In a materialist, capitalist liberal economy where religion has become at most an ironic pastime for many members of the educated middle classes, it can be forgotten that for some groups and persons it is still a central shaping force, not an epiphenomenon. This is graphically illustrated by the encounters of Afro-Caribbean people with psychiatrists in this country. What Afro-Caribbeans take to be the expression of appropriate religious sentiments can be taken by psychiatrists as symptomatology – with disastrous effects for their reluctant patients.[5] Religion round the world is not a spent force – most of the world's population is still overtly religious.[6] Religiously formed and committed people continue to form a substantial and influential social group in this country. They deserve to be understood as much as any other minority group. Understanding how religion functions for people and groups in terms of content, context, practice and world-view is an important part of seeking health and well-being.

There is a certain inevitability about religion in human life. For whatever reason (psychological need, social cohesion, etc.), individuals and groups feel the need to construct metaphors, myths, symbols, rituals and communities of practice which have some kind of transcendent reference and give shape and coherence to personal and social life. Arguably, no one escapes being bound up in some kind of religious/theological system if one accepts Geertz's definition that religion is:

> (1) a system of symbols which acts to (2) establish powerful, pervasive, and long-lasting moods and motivations in men by (3) formulating conceptions of a general order of existence and (4) clothing these conceptions with such an aura of factuality that (5) the moods and motivations seem uniquely realistic.[7]

The challenge for all seeking human well-being is to recognize this religious component of existence and to see how it can be integrated into an overall quest for human flourishing. The practical theologian, as a self-conscious and critical 'insider' of a particular religious community of faith, metaphor, etc., has several useful things to contribute in this quest as (a) artist and critic of belief, myth, metaphor and symbol; (b) practitioner of transformational and reflective knowledge; (c) purveyor of distinctively theologically-derived methods, concepts and insights.

(a) Artist and critic of belief, myth, metaphor and symbol

Bernard Walsh, David Lodge's hero in *Paradise News*, may have despaired because no one was interested in theology except fellow professional theologians. Clearly, his vision of the pervasiveness of theology and religious symbols was too narrow. As he later discovers, paradise as a guiding myth of purposeful pilgrimage is what fuels the tourist industry. If he had wandered into the public sector of the British welfare system he would have found it similarly full of powerful myths, metaphors and symbols. (Arguably, indeed, the last decade in Britain has been composed of a theological revolution – witness Mrs Thatcher's 'Sermon on the Mound'. Unfortunately, most theologians missed the theological nature of this revolution and so proved poor critics of it.) Even in such apparently finite and concrete activities as health promotion, ostensibly firmly based on scientific findings about the causes of disease, there is a real sense in which understanding seeks after faith. It is, for example, one thing to know that 35 per cent of cancers are diet-related, but quite another to know who will contract them, where and when. In asking people to change their individual dietary habits one is asking them to put their trust in extrapolations from experts' interpretations of scientific findings. Upon such acts of faith are individuals' world-views changed or confirmed, and government policies determined.

One of the advantages of a theological training is that one can recognize the symbols, myths and metaphors of a faith system when one sees one, whether it be in medicine or in social policy.[8] In the case of the latter, we are clearly in a situation where the manufacture of action-guiding metaphors is at a high premium. Within the overarching myths and metaphors of the free market economy (itself sustained by the belief of ordinary people) there is a veritable industry manufacturing meanings, visions and symbols which are supposed to motivate people and guide the direction of organizations.[9] The language of apocalyptic is rife as people throw out mission statements, doom scenarios and metaphors of chaos and order. The rediscovery of values and meaning lies at the heart of the management revolution which has swept through public service as well as private industry in the last decade or so.[10] Peters and Waterman, for example, wax lyrical as they claim that 'so much excellence in performance has to do with people's being motivated by compelling, simple – even beautiful – values'.[11] They suggest that 'good managers make meanings for people, as well as money',[12] and they argue that 'Instead of brain games in the sterile ivory tower, it's shaping values (management's job becomes more fun) through coaching and evangelism in the field – with the worker and in support of the cherished product'.[13] The company or organization should become a community of the faithful, finding meaning and productivity together as they colonize an ever-expanding future and wrest from it blessing for themselves and their customers. Having developed their key values, the point is then to act, for actions speak louder than words and, of course, they reinforce faith.[14] The faith of the managers can be summarized as 'I believe, therefore I can do'.[15]

Unfortunately, most of the charismatic organizational prophets who are so keen to coin and commend snappy organizing metaphors which give order, meaning and direction to life seem largely uncritical of the dangers and limitations of this activity (for example, the metaphor of mission may have unwanted connotations of dualism, 'us and them' thinking and legitimate aggression). Theologians, as self-conscious purveyors, interpreters and users of metaphors and symbols such as these, can be useful here in drawing attention to the disclosive possibilities of words, concepts and faith systems, interrogating them and dialoguing them with others in such a way that they are not uncritically accepted as straightforward descriptions of reality.

Perhaps most importantly, theologians who are aware of the reifying, idol-creating possibilities of language in talking about God can continue to remind people of the limits of language and the inexhaustibility of explanation. There is no one discourse or set of metaphors with explanatory power which does not exclude other ways of seeing and describing. Our knowledge of reality, as of God, is partial, fragmentary and ever changing. Marking boundaries to the 'totalizing' potential of human discourses is of vital importance in a world where a mixture of pragmatism and ideology can easily be mistaken for the totality of all that is.

At their best and most creative, theologians may be able to suggest better, more comprehensive, or more adequate metaphors and symbols for guiding individual and social processes which tend more to the desired good and avoid unfortunate side-effects. In his novel *The Gift of Stones*, Jim Crace describes the delicate process of making flint blades.[16] First, stones of good potential are selected, then they are heated, then they are deftly struck by a craftsman who, as it were, discloses the blade which was already contained in or implicit in the rock. So with the theologian, there is an element of artistic craft which can hew from the word-face illuminating, multifaceted metaphors which can help to orient and give meaning to life and activity. There is more than a little of the poetic and artistic about religious and theological discourse, which can provide the sort of 'soft knowledge' which people appear to need to order their lives and activities. The language of longing and desire is part of describing reality and human motivation adequately. It deserves more explicit attention in most contemporary endeavours worthy of human participation.

If we live by metaphors, myths and symbols, and these structure our lives and institutions with their implicit teleologies and ontologies, then the task of analysing the faith systems pervading the world in which we live and the various activities we undertake is a vital and central service, not just an optional extra for the theologically marginal and unemployed. The discourse of devices and desires, hopes and fears, which is so familiar to theologians, can have an important critical function beyond the narrow sphere of the specifically religious and theological. If this kind of analysis and engagement can be supplemented by adding in to discussions about human well-being new and more creative metaphors and symbols, then theology can be a very useful partner in helping to educate and attain human flourishing.

(b) Practitioner of transformational and reflective knowledge

The mention of 'soft knowledge' above brings me on to the role of the theologian in purveying transformational knowledge. Increasingly, we are living in an environment where all activity must be measured and must be clearly describable in terms of actual behaviour (hence the emphasis on skills and competencies which can be observed in many activities). Vague concepts of 'education' are giving way to much more limited and concrete ideas of training which is designed to produce particular skills and competencies for specific roles. However, at the very moment when a ratio-technocratic view of life seems about to triumph, the realization that not everything can be reduced to these terms is beginning to emerge. Senior managers in the public sector are starting to show an interest in nebulous topics such as ethics, and want to develop skills of judgement and discernment which are not easily categorizable. Some nurses are revolting against the idea that all their activity can be reduced to itemizable and separable acts — the actual task of nursing, they say, is more than the sum of its separate parts.[17]

Lying behind this kind of protest is the quest for what can be called 'transformational knowledge':

> Transformational knowledge involves intuition, wisdom, and mystery in contrast to technical control . . . Transformational knowledge is a peculiar amalgam, different from the methodological knowledge sought by the humanities in their academic and scholarly pursuits. Members of the transformational disciplines are always faced with the 'messy' aspects of human life.[18]

This kind of transformational knowledge emanates in large part from the transitional realm of the symbol, where reason and emotion, conscious and unconscious intersect and interconnect to generate fundamental, if not necessarily verbally articulatable, understandings, hopes, fears and world-views. It is in this dimension that religion operates and from which it gains its importance and significance if psychoanalytic theorists are to be believed.[19]

The point about transformational knowledge is not just that it is messy, and in a sense amounts to informal knowledge, personal knowledge and that elusive thing, 'wisdom' (the kind of knowledge which is very difficult to evaluate and assess by any kind of examination process). It is also knowledge which arises to a large extent from people's experience of living. It is knowledge directed towards actually changing or transforming people. American psychologist of religion Paul Pruyser writes 'It has always been the business of the religio-theological enterprise to *transform* people, not just to *know* what people are'.[20]

Clearly, practical theologians are not the only group who have to do with transformational knowledge (Pruyser believes most groups which have to try and make meliorative interventions, e.g. psychiatrists and social workers, have to work with this kind of knowledge). However, theologians have the possible advantage of standing within a long tradition of using and reflecting upon this kind of knowledge in order to help people achieve their potential. They have taken this kind of knowledge very seriously (having not had the benefit of hard, objective, arm's length scientific knowledge), and this endows them with experience and reflective skills which may help them to meet the demand for training in wisdom and virtue which is now becoming very audible.

It could reasonably be argued that philosophers, and particularly ethicists, have as much to contribute here as theologians. While this may be true in theory, in practice modern philosophy has frequently lost touch with the quest for the integration of action and transformational knowledge in the wise person. Philosophers, even so-called 'applied philosophers', are confined within a paradigm of rationalistic analysis, detached from action and the wider community within the academy. They are not necessarily practitioners of their own ideas or involved in practical action within communities or outside the academy. Curiously, one of the last repositories of the search for wisdom and following through thought in personal and corporate character and action is the religious community. The experience of trying to do this is now of value in the secularized world.

(c) Purveyor of distinctively theologically-derived methods, concepts and insights

I have left until last the more specific aspects of theological content and method which can be contributed to the general quest for human well-being. This is to re-emphasize the point I made earlier, that very overtly religious questions and techniques can only appropriately be introduced into wider secular discussion with great discretion, lest they seem intrusive, evangelistic or obfuscatingly 'theological' in the pejorative, mystifying sense of the word.

One set of techniques which can find favour with a wide audience is that of critical hermeneutic method. The interpretation of ideas, events and persons is another important aspect of the 'soft knowledge' of reality, which I have suggested is becoming ever more important in seeking to intervene usefully to nurture human flourishing. The extensive expertise of theologians in trying to discern action-guiding interpretations from texts is also applicable on a much larger stage, and can help to loose people from narrow, monolithic or unduly pragmatic understandings of reality.

Some of the basic questions which form the horizons of theological enquiry can form a similarly useful critical framework for practitioners and others attempting to discern directions for action. To help people to stand back and ask questions such as 'What are our fundamental understandings of life and its purpose?', 'To what end do we tend?', 'Are we the beginning and end of our own existences?', 'To what extent are we responsible for our events which take place in the world?' and 'How do we cope with failure and the inability to accomplish our good intentions satisfactorily?' is a useful function which can be welcomed in situations where utilitarian pragmatism and fragmentation has come to dominate a good deal of discourse. (This last question is a particularly pertinent one in British public service at the moment, where the gospel of high-morale success is preached by managers who lack the resources to implement their visions, and where dissent and criticism is being increasingly viewed as disloyalty.) Interestingly, these large and apparently abstract questions seem to be practically liberating for many people who begin to perceive their thought and action within a much wider context.

Finally, there are distinctively theological insights arising from the community of faith, the consideration of which can be of service. So, for example, the concept of mission, so beloved now throughout the secular world, can be greatly illuminated, and its strengths and limitations assayed, by consideration of the Christian community's experience of mission (a very ambivalent one). Or the nature of social institutions can be usefully critiqued from the perspective of Christian ideas about spirits and demons.

To elaborate a little further on this second example, Walter Wink, a New Testament scholar, suggests from his researches that heavenly powers or spirits always have a material and an immaterial aspect.[21] Thus, the various churches of the Revelation of St John the Divine have an outward aspect (their embodied members, the place where they meet, etc.), but there is also a 'spirit' of the church which manifests its ethos. This consideration of material and non-material reality is enormously illuminating when applied to organizations such as hospitals, as it helps us to grasp and take seriously the 'feel' of the place as well as its outward realities (e.g. number of staff, management systems, etc.) Workers within the 'harder' social sciences find it difficult to lay hold upon and analyse what is a pervasive and important yet elusive 'spirit of place'. To do the complexity of reality justice, it is just this spirit which must be taken into account, rather than allowing it to be dismissed because it is intangible and cannot be surveyed or measured.

Doubtless, this kind of example might serve to justify the worst fears of an emancipated liberal academic who might see it as an attempt to re-sacralize or re-demonize the world. This underlines the need to be sparing in one's overt use of theological insights and concepts. However, it is important to note how useful and real the 'soft knowledge' provided by theological study actually can be in encountering social reality and system.

Conclusion

I hope I have now said enough to establish the usefulness of theological training, methods and insights outwith the narrow confines of academic theology as it is presently conceived and studied. With its roots in the symbolic, transformative, reflective 'soft' knowledge of the community of faith, theology is in an excellent position to remind people of the extent, significance and nature of historical and contemporary religious belief and practice. It can have an enormously positive role in pointing up and helping people to negotiate the forest of symbols, myths and meanings which permeate all aspects of human life with critical commitment. It can also contribute helpfully to myth analysis and manufacture, as well as to the quest of disclosing the limits and possibilities of the metaphors we live by. Finally, from the content of theology can be derived critical concepts which can question and modify conceptualizations and practices over a wide range of human activity.

Whether or not I have succeeded in substantiating my case, it behoves me to make a few final qualifying remarks before I issue a twofold concluding challenge to theologians and non-theologians in the academy.

First, I must re-emphasize that this has been a solipsistic and functional account of the usefulness of theology, based on my own experience and activity. Others will have had other experiences and will be able to suggest other ways in which theology can be made more useful.

Secondly, it may rightly be argued that many of the tasks which I have suggested for theology and theologians could be contributed by practitioners of other disciplines from which theology has drawn, e.g. literary criticism, linguistic theory, philosophy, psychoanalysis. I would not want to contest this for one moment. I would only say that theology combines many of these methods and insights together in a distinctive way which is directly related to practice and ordinary living.

Thirdly, there is a danger that I have exaggerated some aspects of the contribution of theology, while minimizing or completely omitting others. I could not rebut this criticism, except by saying that what I have attempted here is a functional and personal rather than a systematic or comprehensive account.

Finally, some might accuse me of reinventing the wheel. Theologians like David Jenkins, for example, have long been engaged in trying to pay close attention to human flourishing, and to introducing elements of linguistic analysis and theological critique into the secular sphere of, for example, the National Health Service. That this is so is both irrefutable and welcome. However, there is scope for many people to reflect upon and engage in this kind of activity, from many directions. I have simply recorded my own preliminary reflection on my own involvement, in the hope that it is better for the wheel to be reinvented rather than completely forgotten or discarded. So, then, to my positive challenges to theologians and non-theologians in the academy.

To the theologians, I say: Your training, disciplines and methods could certainly contribute more directly and more usefully on a wider stage. However, this will require changes both in the way that theologians regard themselves and their relationships, and in the way that they conduct and communicate themselves. Contrary to most leading theologians (practical and other), I have to assert that theology must be willing to come to regard itself not just as servant of the church and Christian community, a kind of critical feedback mechanism for Christian practice alone, but must see itself as serving wider human concerns and interests.[22] This does not necessarily mean breaking connections with communities of faith (these, after all, are source of part of the knowledge and skill base which theology distinctively offers). It does, however, entail a willingness to engage with broader agendas and concerns in a more serious and direct way.

I do not think that this is unreasonable to ask or impossible to perform. The current shape of academic theology owes more to accident and historical precedent than it does to any self-conscious deliberation about what theological and human priorities should be. There is no reason why this should not change. And along with this, there is no reason why theologians should not make more effort to interpret themselves, their insights and methods to a wider audience whose concerns are more directly addressed. It is surely time for theologians to apply hermeneutic principles to their own discourse, in the belief that if something is worth saying it is worth saying it in such a way that non-theologians can appreciate its worth and significance. (A friend of mine who ran a theological college banned the use of the word 'theology' and that of theological technical jargon for a term in his college, on the grounds that these were often used ideologically, obfuscatingly, and as a substitute for more widely intelligible communication!) For the sake of theology itself, theology must resist becoming a private language, for private languages inevitably decay, die and are forgotten.

To those who regard themselves as non-theologians and who may regard this discipline as systematized and partisan superstition, I would say two things. First, are you quite sure that you do not yourselves have implicit hopes, fears, mythologies, theologies and belief systems in your own disciplines which could not benefit from self-conscious theological interrogation and insights? Secondly, is it not about time that those disciplines which have emancipated themselves from the historic control and distortions of religion preceding the Enlightenment had the self-confidence to critically assimilate and learn from the insights and methods which theology has to offer? Modern liberal theology is interrogative, critical and increasingly powerless institutionally; it does not deserve continuing demonization.

If theological and non-theological disciplines can find some willingness to listen respectfully to each other and to change a little along the lines which I have tentatively suggested it is possible that, far from being useless, theology could come to be perceived as very useful indeed.

Notes

1. David Lodge, *Paradise News* (London: Secker and Warburg, 1991), p. 29.
2. David Tracy, *The Analogical Imagination* (London: SCM Press, 1981).
3. Paul Lehmann argues that the purpose of Christianity itself is that of 'making and keeping human life human in the world'. See Paul L. Lehmann, *Ethics in a Christian Context* (New York: Harper and Row, 1976).
4. Duncan B. Forrester, *Christianity and the Future of the Welfare State* (London: Epworth, 1985).
5. Roland Littlewood and Maurice Lipsedge, *Aliens and Alienists: Ethnic Minorities and Psychiatry* (London: Unwin Hyman, 1989).
6. Rex Ambler, *Global Theology* (London: SCM Press, 1990).
7. C. Geertz, 'Religion as a cultural system', quoted in Roger Cooter, *The Cultural Meaning of Popular Science* (Cambridge: Cambridge University Press, 1984), p. 368, n. 86.
8. It is doubtful whether any meaningful human activity can take place without some kind of guiding mythology to inform and integrate it. Campbell notes four main functions for myths. These are (1) the awakening and maintenance in the individual of a sense of awe in the face of ultimate mystery; (2) the rendering of a cosmology which makes the world intelligible; (3) the validation and maintenance of social order; (4) the centring and harmonization of the individual. If he is right, then clearly mythology is omnipervasive. The engagement of theology with all these areas has been and should continue to be significant, thus making it highly relevant. See further Joseph Campbell, *The Masks of God: Creative Mythology* (London: Penguin, 1976), ch. 9.
9. David Jenkins, 'False gods and false accounting' in *Free to Believe* (London: BBC, 1991), ch. 8.
10. Stephen Pattison, 'Mystical management: a religious critique of public service management', *Modern Churchperson* 33 (NS), (1991), pp. 17–27.
11. T. Peters and R. Waterman, *In Search of Excellence* (London: Harper and Row, 1982).
12. lbid., p. 37.
13. lbid., p. 29.
14. Ibid., p. xxv.
15. Ibid., p. 74.
16. Jim Crace, *The Gift of Stones* (London: Pan Books, 1989).
17. See further, e.g. Elizabeth Hart, 'Ghost in the machine', *Health Service Journal* 101.5281 (1991), pp. 20–2.
18. John R. Patton, *From Ministry to Theology* (Nashville: Abingdon, 1990), p. 70. For more on the concepts of 'transformational knowledge' and 'soft knowledge' see Donald A. Schon, *The Reflective Practitioner* (Aldershot: Avebury, 1991).
19. See further, e.g. H. Newton Maloney and Bernard Spilka (eds), *Religion in Psychodynamic Perspective* (New York: Oxford University Press, 1991); James W. Jones, *Contemporary Psychoanalysis and Religion* (New Haven: Yale University Press, 1991).
20. Quoted in Patton, op. cit., p. 69.
21. Walter Wink, *Unmasking the Powers* (Philadelphia: Fortress Press, 1986).
22. See, e.g. Duncan B. Forrester, 'Divinity in use and practice' in Duncan B. Forrester (ed.), *Theology and Practice* (London: Epworth, 1990). Forrester writes: 'Practical Theology is, in my opinion, a churchly discipline' (p. 9).

4

'God' in the couch? Dare we speak of God in therapeutic counselling?

Emmanuel Lartey

> Fictions, illusions, opinions are perhaps the most intangible and unreal things we can think of; yet they are the most effective of all in the psychic and even the psychophysical realm. (C. G. Jung)[1]

The annals of *TIME* magazine have it that its most famous cover line consists of three words which appeared in April 1966: 'Is God Dead?' The cover caused quite a sensation, including innumerable phone protests and a then record 3,430 letters to the editor. That controversy, it might be noted, was far overshadowed in 1979 by their selection of Ayatollah Khomeni as Man of the Year, which drew 14,180 protests. On 29 November 1993, *TIME*'s cover had a picture of Sigmund Freud, bald head partly taken apart in jigsaw puzzle fashion, with the cover line 'Is Freud Dead?' revisiting the wording concept and the theological controversies of the 1960s, in which Freud's views played no small part. Freud, of course, unlike the deity, actually died in London on 23 September 1939. *TIME* cover writer Paul Gray says 'the Freud story, like the cover on God, examines a system of thought that is a matter of belief for millions but is coming under a particularly blistering attack at the moment'.

The title of this chapter, similarly, is a play on words and concepts which have to do with interactions between, on the one hand, the theory and practice of therapeutic counselling which, to a large extent, owes its origins to the life and work of Sigmund Freud, and, on the other hand, theological speech and thought. The historical fortunes of traditional ideas in both 'God-talk' and 'talking cures' offer much food for thought. The present climate of critique of Freudian thought, and indeed of psychotherapy in general, parallels earlier and ongoing criticism of religious thought and practice, thus enabling a new internal as well as mutual criticism which might yield important results for both.

Now, of course, much has been written about psychoanalysis and religion, and I am certainly not going to be able to survey all of that in this short chapter. Nor am I intending to discuss the numerous assorted pieces of writings by Freud specifically on religion. An interesting and useful recent short survey was published in 1993 by the Freud Museum, entitled *Is Psychoanalysis Another Religion?*,[2] in which an international selection of contemporary clinicians and theoreticians such as David Black, Julia Kristeva, Joel Kovel and Neville Symington explore some of the many relationships that psychoanalysis can have with religion. James Jones, in *Contemporary Psychoanalysis and Religion*,[3] following very much the tradition and approach of Erich Fromm,[4] challenges the domination of Freudian perspectives on religious experience in the psychotherapeutic world, and, while not debunking the entire Freudian heritage, shows how more recent models of personhood, therapy and transference such as those of Fairbairn, Klein, Kohut, and Winnicott, *inter alia*, may demonstrate the relevance of clinical experience for religious studies while also helping the clinician grasp the roles religion may play in human life.

In this chapter it will be my concern to discuss attitudes and responses to 'God-talk' in therapeutic counselling, restricting myself to counselling which draws inspiration from psychoanalytic sources. I shall also attempt to suggest alternative approaches which might enable deeper engagement between some of the processes of therapeutic counselling and forms of theological thinking. Three main assumptions underlie what I shall be presenting:

(1) That many people, in secular (or perhaps post-secularized), modern (or perhaps post-modern), industrialized (or perhaps post-industrialized) Western society, have within them images and concepts of God which have some influence on their personal and relational lives.[5] The influence being spoken of here may be in the form of a reaction against, or a rejection of, images encountered in early life.

(2) That persons engaged in counselling with a therapeutic end in view would do well to give careful attention to *every* inner 'object' which may affect their well-being.

(3) That the goal in view may be served by more serious dialogue between counsellors, psychotherapists and people interested in 'God-talk'.

Largely as a result of Freudian approaches to religious thinking and experience, there exists in psychotherapeutic circles a hesitation about 'God-talk'. Freud gave a classic summary of his views in 1933:

> Religion is an attempt to master the sensory world in which we are situated by means of the wishful world which we have developed within us as a result of biological and psychological necessities. But religion cannot achieve this. Its doctrines bear the imprint of the times in which they arose, the ignorant times of the childhood of humanity. Its consolations deserve no trust. Experience teaches us that the world is no nursery. The ethical demands on which religion seeks to lay stress need, rather, to be given another basis; for they are indispensable to human society and it is dangerous to link obedience to them with religious faith. If we attempt to assign the place of religion in the evolution of mankind, it appears not as a permanent acquisition but as a counterpart to the neurosis which individual civilized men have to go through in their passage from childhood to maturity.[6]

Numerous comments, criticisms, reformulations and rebuttals of Freud's views have been made. My purpose in this chapter is not to rehearse what for many will be fairly familiar debates. I wish simply at this point to draw attention to the legacy that has resulted in a hesitancy about religion in the practice of psychotherapy. For if 'God-talk' is infantile, wishful thinking, primitive, untrustworthy, transitory, neurotic and immature, then surely 'civilized men' would want nothing to do with it. By focusing on the rather dismissive and dogmatic stance manifest in this particular quotation, much of value in the processes of therapy initiated by Freud was lost both to therapists and religionists. It is important to point out that there are many practising psychoanalysts who are also deeply religious people. However, the place of religion in therapy and the treatment of therapy as religion has received relatively little careful consideration.

Carl Jung, Freud's apostate heir apparent, as is well known, took a very different view from Freud on religion, seeing it, as the quotation with which I began illustrates, as potentially offering integrative symbols for human well-being. Jung advocated dialogue between psychotherapists and clergy. But here, also, by focusing on Jung's apparently more favourable attitude to religion, the value of the mutual critique implied in his work has been lost to many therapists and religionists.

Erich Fromm's analysis perhaps sums the position up well:

> Freud opposes religion in the name of ethics – an attitude which can be termed 'religious'. On the other hand, Jung reduces religion to a

> psychological phenomenon and at the same time elevates the unconscious to a religious phenomenon.[7]

Fromm's interest in 'the problem' of religion and psychoanalysis, he asserts, is to show that 'to set up alternatives of either irreconcilable opposition or identity of interest is fallacious'. Instead he suggests that the relation between the two is 'too complex to be forced into either one of these simple and convenient attitudes'.[8] Fromm proceeds by arguing that theistic, non-theistic and secular forms of religion may be either *authoritarian* or *humanitarian*. Indeed, aspects of a particular religious tradition may be authoritarian whilst others may be humanitarian.

The main feature of authoritarian religion is the postulation of a power outside and above human beings which by virtue of its having control over humanity requires obedience, reverence and worship. Authoritarian religious experience then entails a surrender to a transcending power, whether this be a Father-God, the State or a cause. The main virtue proposed by this type of religion is obedience; the cardinal sin devotees may commit is disobedience. Submission to a powerful authority is the main avenue by which a person escapes from feelings of aloneness and limitation. The prevailing emotions and motivations here are sorrow and guilt, and these are the main emotions employed as motivators for moral action.

Humanistic religion, on the other hand, is centred on humans and their strength and ability. The development of powers of reason, awareness, recognition of limitations as well as potential, love for others as well as self, and the experience of the solidarity of all living beings are the main features of humanistic religion. The core experience of humanistic religion is oneness based on relatedness and love. The virtues are self-realization (not obedience) and the achievement of greatest strength (not the greatest powerlessness). The prevailing emotions and motivations are joy and affirmation.

More recently, Neville Symington of Tavistock Clinic fame has made a similar distinction between *revealed* religion and *natural* religion. Symington argues that psychoanalysis by and large rejects revealed religion but is itself a natural religion. The essential questions addressed by natural religions are ethical ones. How should persons live? What is the right path of life for a person? Symington writes:

> [Revealed] religion is concerned with pleasing God or pleasing gods. Natural religion is concerned with the welfare of man [sic] . . . Freud was very anxious that psychoanalysis be differentiated clearly from revealed religion . . . It is clear to me that the stuff of psychoanalysis is how the

> individual treats himself [sic] and others . . . It is the . . . conviction of this author that psychoanalysis is a natural religion in the making.[9]

Fromm and Symington, therefore, unlike Freud, distinguish between different types of religion in terms of their therapeutic effects upon and concern for the well-being of humankind. Fromm sought to show the value of psychoanalytic thought in demonstrating the psychological, social and political dynamics associated with the development in persons of either authoritarian or humanistic conceptions and experiences of God. He argues that a crucial assertion of psychoanalysis can be couched in the statement of the Dutch philosopher Spinoza: 'What Paul says about Peter tells us more about Paul than it does about Peter.' Our interest, then, in Paul's statements about Peter are really that they may be helpful in our understanding of Paul. Fromm is convinced that one of the most significant contributions to human progress that has been made by psychoanalysis is in the study of the processes of *rationalization*. Psychoanalysis unearths the importance of unconscious motivations, together with the place of emotional, social and cultural forces in all thinking and systems of thought. Fromm writes:

> Any idea is strong only if it is grounded in a person's character structure. No idea is more potent than its emotional matrix. The psychoanalytic approach to religion then aims at the *understanding of human reality behind thought systems*. It inquires whether a thought system is expressive of the feeling which it portrays or whether it is a rationalization hiding opposite attitudes.[10]

While acknowledging the difficulty of analysing thought systems, he argues that inconsistencies and contradictions within such systems usually point to discrepancies between consciously held opinion and underlying feeling and, therefore, that these are an important starting point. Thus the way a person looks at his neighbour or talks to a child, the way he eats, walks, or shakes hands, or the way in which a group behaves towards minorities, may be 'more expressive of faith . . . than any stated belief'.[11] It is this attentiveness to the human realities which are associated with 'God-talk'; this attempt to elucidate the emotional origins or concomitants of theological thinking, which constitute an important and necessary task for therapeutic counselling.

What, then, are the aims of therapy? Fromm considers that what is aimed at through psychoanalytic therapy is to help patients achieve, in his terms, a humanistic religious attitude in which they are enabled 'to see truth, to love, to become free and responsible, and to be sensitive to the voice of conscience'.[12] Two therapeutic outcomes are deemed most desirable, namely *freedom* (or individuality) and *independence* (or autonomy) for the client.

It is, perhaps, on these grounds that Fromm's analysis, based as it is on a critical adoption of Freudian and Jungian perspectives, can be criticized. What does it mean to be free? How free can we really be? How independent, and independent of what or whom? Such questions reveal the cultural and philosophical relativity, indeed boundedness, of these therapeutic aims. However, as we shall see, these aims are by no means shared by all therapists.

Until relatively recently, most psychoanalytic investigations of religion have taken place in either a Freudian or a Jungian framework. However, it is increasingly being recognized that post-Freudian and post-Jungian models of psychoanalytic understanding have much to contribute to the discussion. Many contemporary approaches to personality dynamics begin with interpersonal experience rather than with the individual as a self-contained unit of instinctual or archetypal forces. Psychopathology here is seen as arising from the processes of interaction rather than from conflicts generated by repressed biological energies.[13] These newer models shift the focus of psychoanalytic understanding from the *free*, *independent* and isolated individual to the *interactive person made up of internalized interpersonal experiences*. It is these internalized patterns of interaction, rather than biological drives or universal themes, which are expressed in our everyday behaviour, including our 'God-talk' or avoidance of 'God-talk'.

Post-Freudian and post-Jungian approaches, precisely because of their interpersonal orientation, offer insights about the nature of the relationship between counsellor and client – the so-called therapeutic alliance – or in psychodynamic terms the *transference*. In all approaches to therapeutic counselling, the relationship between client and counsellor is reckoned to be crucial to the achievement of the goals of the process. Transference is the technical name given to the phenomena of the client/counsellor relationship. It involves the coming to life of past relationships in the context of the therapeutic relationship. I shall return to the therapeutic encounter later.

W. R. D. Fairbairn and Melanie Klein, representing the so-called 'British' and 'English' schools of object relations respectively, were in the forefront of fairly radical revisions of psychoanalytic theory and practice.[14] Fairbairn is clear that 'a relationship with an object and not the gratification of an impulse is the ultimate aim of libidinal striving'.[15] David Black explains:

> What is meant by 'object-relations' is relations, both real and imagined, with 'significant others'. The mother, as the 'primary object' of most newborn humans, is seen as having a quite special importance, but the father, siblings, teachers and so on are all 'objects', to use this language, and play

crucial roles in building up the new person's capacity to experience the world and to fulfil his or her potentials.[16]

Our primary motivation, according to Fairbairn, then, is to establish object relations, and our personality is structured around the internalization of these relations. Understanding personality means understanding the processes by which external object relations become the internal structures of personality. Understanding a person means grasping the world of his or her inner object relations. In this respect, it is important to note that what is internalized is the emotional tone of the parent–child bond rather than the parent as a static object. It is, for example, the experience of rejection, persecution or unresponsiveness in the relation with the caretaker or parent that is internalized and in this case repressed. Melanie Klein argues that in an attempt to rid ourselves of 'bad objects' (relations) we project them onto the external world in a process she calls 'projective identification'. These same projective mechanisms are at work in the transference in therapy, with the therapist being given the role of unavailable father, overbearing mother, competing elder brother etc.

Heinz Kohut uses the term 'selfobject' to refer to those relationships through which we are enabled to maintain cohesion, vitality, strength and harmony. In spite of the somewhat misleading term, Kohut is speaking about a particular kind of relationship which enhances a strong sense of self. For Kohut, total independence is not possible, for 'a move from dependency (symbiosis) to independence (autonomy) is an impossibility . . . the developmental moves of normal psychological life must be seen in the changing nature of the relationships between the self and its selfobjects'.[17] Thus the human needs for dependency, connection, affirmation, even symbiosis, are never left behind, just transformed into more mature forms. Kohut's basic view is that a self can never exist outside a matrix of selfobjects. We are interconnected, part of a larger matrix. With ideas similar to general systems theory, though stated in very different language, Kohut sees painful interpersonal relations, and not conflict between intrapsychic structures, as being at the root of our problems. By providing a 'second chance' to examine and experience the selfobject matrix within which one may be engaged, therapy may provide an opportunity for growing new, more mature structures. The agent of change, for Kohut, is not interpretation and insight but the relationship between client and therapist itself. This theme of the relational self and the need for interpersonal models is clearly articulated in several feminist writings.[18]

Jones offers an interesting attempt to understand these developments in terms of the dialectics of cultural evolution when he writes:

> Freud and modernity typify the necessary discovery of individuality and autonomy after the medieval symbiosis; Kohut represents the postmodern need to rediscover connection and communion in a way that does not undermine autonomy and individuality but continues a genuine evolution beyond both the enmeshments of medieval society and the brittle autonomies of modernity.[19]

A psychoanalytic investigator who has approached religion in terms of the processes of object relations is Ann Marie Rizzuto. Rizzuto, on the basis of research on the developmental histories of several families, suggests that everyone has some image of God. For some, the image is rejected as an object of faith. For others, it is an object of devotion. These images are 'created from representational materials whose source are the representations of primary objects'.[20] For Rizzuto, images of God are created out of the experience of the mother. She follows Winnicott in locating the reality of God in the 'transitional space', the realm of imagination out of which the child creates a private but real world from transitional objects such as teddy bears, security blankets, imaginary friends and magical beliefs. This imaginary capacity, the world of fantasy and abstract ideas, Rizzuto argues, demands our respect rather than ridicule, for it has a powerful effect on our mental health and psychological well-being. 'We have forgotten', she writes, 'the powerful reality of nonexistent objects, objects of our creation . . . The fictive creations of our minds have as much regulatory potential in our psychic function as people around us in the flesh.'[21]

Rizzuto makes a distinction between 'God' and all other transitional objects. The main difference between God and all other transitional objects lies in the fact that the others are eventually outgrown or put away. But because God is not an experimental object, and because the image of God, unlike teddy bears or favourite bits of clothing, is infinitely plastic, a person may throughout life 'create' a God according to their needs. Rizzuto is convinced that whether a person becomes an atheist or a believer is influenced by whether or not the person's image of God fits or can be reworked to fit their need at any given developmental stage in their life. As an example she refers to the experience of one of her subjects whose image of God was shot through with masochistic rage and destructive anger, as a result of the subject's experience of his father. This subject became increasingly unable to do anything with this image as he grew older, and eventually rejected any idea of God because the pain associated with it was intolerable.

Rizzuto can be faulted for focusing unduly on transitional objects, rather than on the transitional experience as Winnicott, whom I will be discussing in greater detail shortly, does; and on internalized objects more than on internalized relationships, which as we have seen were the main point made by both Fairbairn and Kohut. Thus she makes God sound like a supernal teddy bear created entirely by the imagination of a child, who for some obscure reason is never really left behind. The strength, however, of her approach lies in the fact that it enables us to examine the way imagination and early parental experience operate in the constructions of God we encounter in the lives of many people. Moreover, her attention to developmental stages arguably finds support in the work of faith developmentalists such as James Fowler.[22]

William Meissner, in an illuminating book entitled *Psychoanalysis and Religious Expcrience*, takes our thinking further on the subject of object relations as applied to religious ideation and experience. Meissner, like Rizzuto, makes use of the influential work of the British paediatrician and psychoanalyst D. W. Winnicott. Meissner first undertakes a psychoanalytic study of Freud's atheism, concluding that Freud's religious views 'reflected at every step deep psychological forces and unresolved conflicts within his psychic economy'.[23] Thus he shows that, just as there may be neurotic reasons for believing in God, so there may be neurotic reasons for refusing such belief. In so doing, Meissner demonstrates the value of psychoanalytic studies of thought systems in general and religious thinking in particular. Erik Erikson has, similarly, arguably shown this value in his 'psychohistories' of religious figures like Luther and Gandhi.[24] Meissner follows Winnicott in applying notions of transitional phenomena to religion. Winnicott's transitional phenomena begin with the infant's experience of mother. He argues that this experience first focuses on the mother's body, especially her breast, and later is carried by specific transitional objects, like blankets and teddy bears, that continue to evoke the maternal experience of soothing and nurturing. Such objects smooth the infant's transition from dependence to independence. Winnicott includes the capacity to play, the exercise of creativity, the use of symbols and the production of art, literature and other works of culture within the ambit of transitional phenomena. Winnicott's 'transitional space' is 'an intermediate area of experiencing, to which inner reality and external life both contribute . . . the intermediate area between the subjective and what is objectively perceived'.[25] Like all transitional phenomena, faith represents a realm in which the subjective and the objective interact. Although the believer brings personal and subjective experience to the process of believing, faith is not entirely subjective. Its contents are affected by the traditions and experiences of others in an organized community, and relate to the nature of the world of human existence, values and spirituality. For Meissner, a person's image of God arises from the tension between their own private experience and the images and metaphors for God provided by their culture. It belongs neither to the individual's private world, nor to the surrounding environment, but rather is a coming together of both. In this he echoes some of the work of Fairbairn, applying it specifically to the concept of God. Guntrip makes Fairbairn's point clearly when he declares 'The inner and outer worlds have a two-way causal relationship and reciprocal influence'.[26] One of the strengths of Meissner's work is that he does not speak in generalized terms about 'religion', but rather focuses on four aspects, namely faith, God representations, symbols and prayer. Moreover, unlike Winnicott he does not stress the functional value of transitional phenomena in providing comfort and evoking creativity, but rather emphasizes the interplay of subjective and objective forces in transitional phenomena and, therefore, the aspects of religion he studies.

Meissner's contribution, then, lies: *firstly*, in his recognition that psychodynamic and neurotic factors similar to those operative in religion can also play a part in atheism or humanism; *secondly*, in the elaboration of adaptive as well as infantile functions of religion; and *thirdly*, in the elucidation, through the use of Winnicott's concept of transitional phenomena, of the interplay of inner subjective and external objective factors in religious thinking and experience.

In January my five-year-old son asked me 'Dad, you're God really, aren't you?' I was obviously interested in finding out the origins of and reasons for the misapprehension. I would like to believe that it had little to do with any particular way of behaving at home on my part. So I asked 'What makes you think that?' 'Well', he replied, indicating part of the origins of his thinking, 'we sing about you in church!' With Advent and Christmas just past, and my particular name, I realized what a perceptive observation he had made. The interaction of inner subjective imagination (God must really be someone we know) with external religious ritual (hymn singing), the importance of symbols (names) and the experience of the parental environment seem to have all played a part in the child's perceptions.

David Black recognizes the value of object relations theory to the appreciation of the role of religious ritual in religious ideation and experience. He argues that religious ritual seeks to create and sustain a world of internal objects, additional to the ones arising spontaneously from a person's own experience, and to foster an 'emotional engagement' or relationship to these objects.[27] Black suggests that for most people the objects derived from experience are always more powerful than those created by religion. Religious 'objects' may thus simply be ignored, or else may contribute to the personal pathology that Freud sees in all religion. However, in some people the objects-of-religion, being more harmonious with the objects-of-experience, become a major strengthening force in their lives, enabling them to gain serenity, self-acceptance, and courage to take risks and endure hardships. Faith in God is, therefore, ambiguous in its results — for some it may result in damaging personal and interpersonal relations, for others it may be a harmonizing and inspiring force for good. Inner dynamics as they interact with social forces, especially in the 'transitional space' of imagination, play, creativity, art, drama and symbolism, result in concepts of God and orientations to life which may be healthy or else destructive.

Theologians, precisely because they are *theo*logians, are interested in the ideas, images, concepts and constructions of God which we encounter in people's experience, in history, in texts, in literature and in other cultural productions. As new historical, social and political situations have demanded, some theologians have re-examined, reformulated or reconstructed the symbol 'God' in response. I am in agreement with Gordon Kaufman's view that:

> The theological imagination devotes itself to the continuing critical reconstruction of the symbol 'God', so that it can with greater effectiveness orient contemporary and future human life.[28]

Theologians most often operate within specific religious traditions. However, some of the more creative and adventurous have sought to cross traditional lines and explore the essence and meaning of 'God-talk' across religious boundaries. What I have been seeking to do in this chapter is to encourage a crossing-over into the world of therapeutic counselling of the psychodynamic kind, to investigate some of the ways in which the encounter with 'God-talk' is being undertaken. There are ways in which certain forms of the theological imagination might be of value to the therapeutic endeavour. Similarly, there are ways in which psychotherapy might contribute to the theological task.

Firstly, I hope I have shown some of the origins of the theological hesitancy on the part of many psychotherapists. I hope it is also clear that I am of the view that this hesitancy may be overcome. If ideas of God belong to the realm of transitional phenomena which are shaped by inner and outer forces interacting primarily, but not exclusively, in the parental environment; and if these concepts may be part of the transferential situation within the therapeutic encounter, then it is crucial that therapists and counsellors be in a position to engage with these 'objects' in imaginative, constructive and, indeed, therapeutic, ways.

Secondly, if theologians are truly interested in the constructions of the symbol 'God' in the experience of human persons; and if these constructions may be examined and may be helpful in the task of reformulating traditional views, then therapists and counsellors may have something to offer theologians.

Thirdly, if theologians have, for centuries, been in the business of critically examining concepts of God, then they may have something to offer therapists in their encounters with ideas and speech of God in the couch.

A question which therapeutic counsellors might find it useful to respond to is: Are you willing and able to engage with the images of and speech about God with which your clients might operate? Many therapists might respond that they do engage with whatever their clients bring up. I have often heard therapists say, though, that they do not feel that it is their place to engage in religious discussions with their clients; that their clients are not there for that purpose. Referrals are often made to more 'competent' people, sometimes sympathetic or psychologically-trained clergypersons. Some counsellors understand pastoral counselling to be the form of counselling most suited for 'religious problems'. The hesitancy still remains.

Further, the lingering feeling that religious thoughts and feelings are pathogenic (anxiety-, guilt-, or illness-producing) in all cases often is tacitly and non-verbally communicated. As is well known, therapy often acts as a subtle form of social influence, with client raising or suppressing material in response to non-verbal cues from therapist, whilst also influencing therapist in non-verbal ways.[29] The establishment of the therapeutic 'bond' which will result in the idiosyncratic relationship between client and counsellor, and enable the client to express and work through the issues and problems that have brought them to therapy, is a crucial task of the therapeutic counsellor. Rapport, empathy, warmth and genuineness are identified as the crucial relational characteristics of effective counselling.[30]

Psychotherapists have shown themselves amenable to the most stringent and strident criticism, as a recent book edited by Professor of Counselling Windy Dryden and freelance (eclectic) counsellor Colin Feltham, entitled *Psychotherapy and Its Discontents*, has shown.[31] To my mind the kind of self-criticism engaged upon in this book may actually be a sign of health. Perhaps pastoral care as it exists in and is offered by the churches could do with a dose of this kind of tough self-criticism!

Some questions which theologians, and those who would offer counselling from a theological perspective, might do well to address are: Of what therapeutic value are the processes and formulations of the concept of God you engage in? Is your theology therapeutic? Does it result in health and healing for all? What inner dynamics and outer relational patterns go with your philosophical theologies, devotional exercises and meditational disciplines? What of transformational significance for persons and societies is aimed at or achieved by the constuctions of and relationships with 'God' espoused? Do your concepts and words about God set human persons free from personal, social and political oppression? To use Johannine language: Have you known 'the truth' and has 'the truth set you free'? (John 8.33).

I hope it is clear that my response to the question 'Dare we speak about God in therapeutic counselling?' would be in the affirmative. Yes! but the crucial question is: *what kind of God-talk?*

God-talk in therapeutic counselling, if not in other areas as well, if it is to respond to the challenges posed, may have the following characteristics: it will be

1. *Tentative*

Rather than dogmatic. In this it will reflect the fact that, although God may be Eternal and Unchanging, our language and symbols will always be stammerings. It will perhaps be apophatic, able to recognize what cannot be 'God', while unable to state categorically what is. Eschatological verification, no matter how defensive it may sound, may be the only assurance – and we may discover eschatologically that we were mistaken; but even that, in the unconditional graciousness of God, would not be disastrous.

2. *Provisional*

Not a finished product or a 'given'. For, if God is Infinite, then there can never be a last word on God. Whatever we know or experience of God, 'we see only puzzling reflections in a mirror' (1 Cor 13.12). This does not mean our concepts or symbols are useless, they are, indeed, our only way of being in relationship with the Reality they symbolize. We may have to discard some of them as time goes by, but in the time being they may serve valuable transitional functions.

3. *Poetic*

Instead of propositional. The language of love, rather than that of cold calculation. This point was suggested and illustrated movingly by the Cadbury lecturer for 1990, Professor Rubem Alves, an originator of liberation theology, professor of philosophy in Brazil and psychoanalyst.[32] This language is imaginative, playful and creative.

4. *Exploratory*

On the path of challenge, discovery and adventure. A therapeutic concept of God for me at the moment is that of the *horizon*, which is ever ahead and against which perspectives are taken. As we change our location, the horizon appears to change too (get closer or else recede); but remains our line of orientation, perspective and discernment.

5. *Feeling after*

With creative uncertainty. Psychoanalysis explains that much of the language and representations of Christian faith is the language of longing. The language of fantasy. French professor of linguistics and psychoanalyst Julia Kristeva puts it thus:

> To the analyst ... the representations on which the Credo is based are fantasies, which reveal fundamental desires or traumas but not dogmas. Analysis subjects these fantasies to X-ray examination. It begins by individualizing: What about *your* father? Was he 'almighty' or not? What kind of son were *you*? What about your desire for virginity or resurrection? By shifting attention from the 'macrofantasy' to the 'microfantasy' analysis reveals the underlying sexuality, which prayer circumvents but does not really proscribe; for though the object of desire be transformed, desire itself remains a feature of Christian discourse.[33]

6. *Examining and affirming the 'image of God'*

Leaving no stone unturned in the search for the well-being of humankind.

7. *Experiential*

Taking seriously people's reports and stories of religious experience, as well as the 'non-experience', the *silence* or 'absence of God' in human experience.

8. *Mystery-embracing*

Rather than rationalizing every occurrence and image. Trinitarian formulations, for example, grapple with the unity, transcendence and immanence of God. God is seen to be absolute, humane and present. Kristeva sees this as reflecting deeply the human psyche:

> The Trinity itself, that crown jewel of theological sophistication, evokes, beyond its specific content and by virtue of the very logic of its articulation, the intricate intertwining of the three aspects of psychic life: the symbolic, the imaginary and the real.[34]

9. *Interpersonal*

Encouraging respect and harmony between persons, recognizing that the nature of interpersonal relations is crucial for any healthy religious outlook. If the work of the post-Freudian and post-Jungian analysts we have surveyed is taken seriously, then 'God' is often a relational symbol reflecting early life relationships and desires. The transference, within the interpersonal context of the client–counsellor encounter, may help to elucidate and free this symbol to become healthy and health-giving.

10. *Corporate*

A global and pluralistic affair, listening to voices from many different cultures, realizing that no one people, nation or tradition has a monopoly on truth.

Therapeutic counselling, whether psychologically, psychoanalytically or theologically inspired, instead of tacitly forbidding 'God-talk', or else viewing such talk as necessarily pathogenic, guilt-producing or neurotic, may enable people to articulate and listen attentively, deeply and creatively to all their 'inner objects' with their relational, transitional and transformational consequences.

Notes

1. C. G. Jung (trans. R. F. C. Hull), *Psychology and Western Religion* (London and New York: Routledge, 1988), p. 198.
2. Ivan Ward (ed.), *Is Psychoanalysis Another Religion? Contemporary Essays on Spirit, Faith and Morality in Psychoanalysis* (London: Freud Museum Publications, 1993).
3. James W. Jones, *Contemporary Psychoanalysis and Religion: Transference and Transcendence* (New Haven and London: Yale University Press, 1991).
4. Erich Fromm, *Psychoanalysis and Religion* (New Haven and London: Yale University Press, 1967).
5. The figure given in recent surveys is that approximately 75 per cent of the population in this country claim to believe in 'God'.
6. S. Freud, 'The question of a *Weltanschauung*' in *New Introductory Lectures on Psychoanalysis*, Lecture 35 (London: Penguin, 1988), p. 204.
7. Fromm, op. cit., p. 20.
8. Ibid., p. 9.
9. Neville Symington, 'Is psychoanalysis a religion?' in Ward (ed.), op. cit., pp. 49–56. The quotation is from p. 56.

10. Fromm, op. cit., p. 62.
11. Ibid., p. 63.
12. Ibid., p. 93.
13. For a review of some of these developments, see J. Greenberg and S. Mitchell, *Object Relations in Psychoanalytic Theory* (Cambridge, MA: Harvard University Press, 1983).
14. For a careful, considered and indeed brilliant treatment of both Fairbairn and Klein's work in relation to Freud's thought, see Harry Guntrip, *Personality Structure and Human Interaction* (London: Hogarth Press and the Institute of Psycho-analysis, 1968).
15. W. R. D. Fairbairn, *An Object Relations Theory of Personality* (New York: Basic Books, 1952), p. 50.
16. David Black, 'The relation of psychoanalysis to religion' in Ward (ed.), op. cit., p. 11.
17. Heinz Kohut, *How Does Analysis Cure?* (Chicago: University of Chicago Press, 1984), p. 52.
18. E.g. N. Chodorow, *Feminism and Psychoanalytic Theory* (Yale University Press, 1989); J. Flax, *Thinking Fragments: Psychoanalysis, Feminism and Postmodernism in the Contemporary West* (University of California Press, 1990). See also Janet Sayers, *Mothering Psychoanalysis* (London: Hamish Hamilton, 1991).
19. Jones, op. cit., p. 18.
20. Ann Marie Rizzuto, *The Birth of the Living God* (Chicago: Chicago University Press, 1979), p. 178.
21. Ibid., p. 47.
22. See the works of James Fowler, a fairly accessible one being *Faith Development and Pastoral Care* (Philadelphia: Fortress Press, 1987).
23. W. W. Meissner, *Psychoanalysis and Religious Experience* (Yale University Press, 1984), p. 55.
24. Erik H. Erikson, *Young Man Luther* (New York: W. W. Norton, 1958); and *Gandhi's Truth: On the Origins of Militant Nonviolence* (New York: W. W. Norton, 1969).
25. D. W. Winnicott, *Playing and Reality* (New York: Routledge, 1971), pp. 2–3.
26. Guntrip, op. cit., p. 360.
27. Black, 'The relation of psychoanalysis to religion', op. cit., p. 12.
28. Gordon Kaufman, *The Theological Imagination* (Philadelphia: Westminster Press, 1981), p. 12.
29. The resemblance of psychotherapy to hermeneutics and exegesis of texts, with the interactions between client and therapist being understood as a quest for and transformation of meaning has been argued for by Jerome Frank. See Jerome D. Frank and Julia B. Frank, *Persuasion and Healing: A Comparative Study of Psychotherapy* (3rd edn, Baltimore and London: The Johns Hopkins University Press, 1991), esp. ch. 3. See also Terence J. Tracey, 'The stages of influence in counselling' in Windy Dryden (ed.), *Key Issues for Counselling in Action* (London: Sage, 1989), pp. 63–71.
30. For a useful exploration of aspects of transference in the counselling relationship, for example where the counsellor is seen as 'ideal' or a 'seer', see C. Edward Watkins, Jr, 'Transference phenomena in the counseling situation' in Dryden (ed.), op. cit., pp. 73–84.
31. Windy Dryden and Colin Feltham (eds), *Psychotherapy and Its Discontents* (Buckingham: Open University Press, 1992). Among the issues raised and discussed by practitioners and consumers of psychotherapy in this incisive book are: the inadequacy of research validating the outcomes of psychotherapy; the possibility that therapy is no more effective than no treatment at all; consumers' experience of therapy as harmful; the

mystically self-protective nature of psychotherapy and its culture; the pretentiousness of therapists' explanations; the widespread personal fallibility and exploitativeness of therapists; psychotherapy's anachronistic detachment from new models; and the psychological reductionism which weakens any political credibility that therapy might have. All these, together with issues of schism, conservatism in conflict with innovativeness within and between schools of therapy, purity or eclecticism, the duration of psychotherapy and whether 'counselling' or 'psychotherapy' is appropriate, are faced.
32. See Rubem Alves, *The Poet, the Warrior, the Prophet* (London: SCM Press, 1990).
33. Julia Kristeva, 'In the beginning was love: psychoanalysis and faith' in Ward (ed.), op. cit., p. 37.
34. Ibid.

5
Reading the Bible within the public domain

Paul Joyce

Picture the scene. A golden July evening in Manchester. At Maine Road Stadium the rock group Queen comes on stage, to a roar of appreciation from a crowd of 50,000 fans, gathered in the open air. Half a mile away, at one of the halls of residence of Manchester University, a mere 100 Old Testament scholars have gathered to listen to the distinguished German scholar Otto Kaiser read a paper on the Second Book of Samuel. The sounds of Queen reverberate across the city, and at least a few of the biblical scholars wish they could be at Maine Road. But as Freddie Mercury launches into 'I Want to Break Free', one of the scholars firmly closes the last open window on the music, leaving the window panes to rattle to the rhythm of 'We Are the Champions'. As Professor Kaiser comes to discuss the incident of King David dancing before the Ark of the Lord, he has the presence of mind to add '— as well he might dance this evening!' But the overwhelming sense that this episode conveys is of two worlds, with little in common; those who read and study the Bible being a tiny ghetto-like minority separated from the great bulk of humanity and out of touch with the lives and interests of most of their contemporaries.

In their various ways, the chapters in this book consider the tension between 'God-talk' and public discourse. Numerous questions are raised for modern people about how to respond to religious texts and traditions, and how they are to be interpreted. Is there an insuperable gap between traditional religious expression and modern experience which makes continued public discourse with shared assumptions impossible? Can the texts and traditions of old be appropriated anew, or must they be rejected for ever? Such questions are posed particularly sharply when we consider the place of the Bible in our modern secularized and pluralistic world.

The modern situation has affected the place of the Bible in many ways. In his contribution to the present book, Hugh McLeod draws a clear (albeit nuanced) contrast between the public profile and widespread influence of Christianity in the early years of this century and the rapid decline that has occurred since the 1950s. Within this broad picture, one can chart the eclipse of the Bible as a publicly acknowledged point of reference: whereas once politicians would readily include allusions to biblical incidents in their speeches, few would do so today and hope to retain an audience; many politicians may themselves be practising Christians, as are still a significant number of the general public, but the assumption that British society *as a whole* constitutes a Christian culture has gone. To a remarkable degree society has become secularized and religion privatized. Then there is the modern phenomenon of cultural pluralism. Anyone living in Birmingham, or indeed any of our other major cities, is strongly aware that modern Britain is a complex mix of faiths and ideologies, religious and otherwise. Traditional faiths such as Islam and Sikhism take their place alongside newer phenomena such as New Age movements. The precise influence all this has on the place of the Bible is, of course, not easy to assess – for example, one complicating factor is that the Bible has a place of honour in Islam – but the general effect of cultural pluralism has certainly been further to marginalize the role of the Bible in our society. The lack of a shared value system and a common pool of tradition is all too evident.

Even within the shrinking circle of Christian believers, modernity has had a very considerable impact on the place of the Bible, not least through the way in which it has generally been studied in universities and colleges, including theological colleges and seminaries. I am referring here to the so-called 'historical-critical' approach, in which the Bible is subjected to the same kind of scrutiny as any other ancient literature. This approach has brought many benefits, helping us understand much about the original meaning of biblical material, but it has had negative effects too. In some ways, the Bible has become just another historical text – a relic of a bygone age. Through being placed within its original setting by the critics, it has for many people lost much of its immediate religious impact. And although the Bible has been much illuminated by comparison with the literature of other ancient cultures, from Egypt to Mesopotamia and even beyond, in part this has served only to relativize it.[1] For years historical critics analysed and dissected the Bible (for example, many scholars discerned documentary 'strands' within Genesis), and any sense that it constituted a unified narrative was eroded.

Moreover, there developed a widespread sense that only the experts could interpret the Bible, whilst others, including even many parish clergy, came to feel deskilled. The Bible, which had emerged within the context of the life of God's people, their struggles and their hopes, now often seemed far removed from that life of faith, and thus the functioning of Scripture was undermined and stultified. By the mid-twentieth century a serious crisis had developed about the place of the Bible within the Church, a crisis which was essentially a product of the impact of that same modernity which had, within society as a whole, been a key factor in the rise of secularization and pluralism.

There stands, then, a big question mark against the role in our time of the Bible, no longer a shared point of reference in our society as a whole, and in many ways not even functioning as Scripture within the modern Church. And yet the situation is neither simple nor straightforward. Hugh McLeod has, in the present volume, challenged some easy assumptions about secularization and the privatization of religion in modern England, showing these to be complex and inconsistent phenomena. As he has pointed out, there remain some areas in which the predominance of religious language and rites remains largely unchallenged. One could add other surprising examples, for instance from the world of rock music, where it seems almost mandatory for 'heavy metal' bands to have names drawn from the glossary of apocalyptic, and where, in a very different way, the songs of an internationally popular group like U2 are laced with biblical allusions ('Jacob wrestled the angel', 'One man betrayed with a kiss', etc.) If one may paraphrase the title of the 1993–94 Cadbury Lectures and ask 'Dare we quote the Bible in public?', the answer for some is very definitely in the affirmative.

In their different ways, both Stephen Pattison and Emmanuel Lartey, in their chapters in the present book, speak of the continuing power of myths and metaphors, stories and symbols, to shape the lives both of individuals and of communities. Pattison argues that theologians may yet have a valuable role to play in helping people to negotiate the forest of symbols, myths and meanings which permeate all aspects of human life, and he shows that the language of apocalyptic is alive and well here too, 'as people throw out mission statements, doom scenarios and metaphors of chaos and order'. Lartey, drawing especially upon the work of the post-Freudian and post-Jungian analysts, makes connections between our internalized interpersonal experiences and our 'God-talk' (or, indeed, our avoidance of 'God-talk'!) and illustrates the function of symbols and the production of art, literature and other works of culture within these processes. In these ways, both Pattison and Lartey show that the need for myths and symbols is not something out of which modern humanity may be said to have grown, but rather that these phenomena are close to the heart of what it is to be human. And so we are prompted to reflect on whether there may yet be ways in which the myths and symbols of the Bible may function afresh in our time.

Recent years have seen a proliferation of new approaches and methods in biblical studies – literary approaches, canonical approaches, feminist criticism and so forth.[2] In many cases, these represent responses to the crisis over the functioning of Scripture within the Church outlined earlier, though they also of course represent the further impact of features of modernity upon the reading of the Bible. The range of new approaches is vast and it would be a mistake to impose an artificial unity upon such disparate phenomena. Nevertheless, many of the newer approaches share some important features, the key one for present purposes being a renewed concern for the contemporary meaning and relevance of texts from the perspective of the modern reader – a move away from a preoccupation with what the text meant originally to a revived interest in what the text can legitimately mean now.[3]

Among the exciting features of the new situation is that literary critics are reading the Bible with renewed interest – exciting, not least because this is a case of the Bible finding a new profile in the *public* domain, rather than just within the relatively narrow confines of the Church or the academy. Among best sellers over recent years have been books with titles such as *The Great Code: The Bible and Literature*, *The Literary Guide to the Bible* and *The Book of God: A Response to the Bible*.[4] These and similar recent books are reviewed in the columns of the *Times Literary Supplement* and the *Spectator*, as other books on the Bible rarely are. Through this development, the Bible's status as a 'classic' within Western culture has been enjoying a surprising degree of reinforcement. Another very interesting feature is that such work often owes at least as much to Jewish writers on the Bible, and, indeed, in some cases non-religious writers too, as it does to Christians. Literary approaches to the Bible are many and varied, but one particularly valuable contribution has been the elucidation of the distinctive 'poetics' of biblical writings, the means whereby texts achieve meaning.[5] We are helped to see, for example, how narrative functions, and within it plot, characterization, point of view, and so forth. Sometimes striking similarities to modern literary forms are exposed, whilst in other cases appreciation of the very differences from modern forms can challenge our assumptions and help make the Bible newly accessible and alive. In such ways, literary approaches can help foster a reclamation of the potentially transformative symbols, myths and images of the Bible.

And yet, for all this, the biblical material can still seem remote, alien and hard to access. How can it relate to modern lives? Modern men and women may still need their myths, but how can the biblical material impinge on these modern myths? Recent developments in hermeneutics, that is, the study of interpretation, have helped a certain amount here. In collaboration with many other disciplines, including philosophy, theologians have reflected a good deal on such issues as how meaning is generated in the reading process, and what effects cultural change might have.[6] Another important (and in many ways closely related) development is the bringing of various modern frames of reference to the biblical text, which is then read in the light of these modern questions. In fact, many of the newer approaches in biblical studies represent ways of attempting to do just this. There can be very creative re-readings of the Bible in terms of modern ways of articulating meaning: liberationist, feminist, 'green', psychological and so forth. These can do much to re-establish the relevance of the Bible and its capacity to speak to contemporary concerns. If much of the present book, and, indeed, much of the present chapter, is about bringing theology into the public domain, these reading strategies, which deliberately let the modern world set the agenda, might be described as bringing the public domain into theology.

Talk of reading the Bible in the light of various features of the modern world may worry some traditional believers, of course. It could be imagined that, for believers, a tension between theological and public discourse does not arise in connection with reading the Bible, on the ground that the Bible provides the world of language and ideas within which believers continue to live, even though two millennia have passed since biblical times. Such is, of course, a naïve and unacceptable assumption. The Bible has always been read within particular cultural and intellectual contexts, whether conditioned by Platonist philosophy, feudal society or numerous other factors (though the implications of this have not generally been acknowledged). Positions which claim complete detachment from non-biblical influences (such as some forms of modern fundamentalism) often betray those influences particularly clearly.[7] It is important, then, for believers to be self-aware and self-critical in considering the context of their biblical reading and the aspects of public discourse which most impinge upon it.

Among the features which most characterize Western culture in the late twentieth century, the language of psychology (albeit often diluted and popularized) is one of the most marked. Though few are widely read in the works of Freud, Jung or Klein, and still fewer espouse the work of such pioneers in a thoroughgoing way, the influence of these and other researchers in the field of human psychology seems pervasive. It is not surprising, then, that there have been many attempts to read the Bible in the light of psychological insights, and in the second half of this chapter I wish to consider one such case by way of example.

It is instructive to consider the modern history and current revival of the psychological approach to the book of Ezekiel, an interesting case of the encounter between the Bible and modernity, which illustrates both the promises and the pitfalls which attend such an approach. The first lecture I ever heard on the Bible suggested that Ezekiel suffered from the effects of 'too much Babylonian sun'. At the time, I took this as a throwaway line designed to engage the attention of day-dreaming students. However, I soon learned that there was a long tradition of attempts to explain some of the unusual features of Ezekiel and his book by reference to his mental state, the descriptions used ranging from mere 'eccentricity' right through to 'schizophrenia'. There is indeed much in the book of Ezekiel which demands explanation, whether it is Ezekiel's sitting 'overwhelmed' among the exiles for seven days (3.15), his perplexing dumbness (3.26–27; 24.27; 33.22), or his bizarre 'sign actions' (e.g. 4.4ff., where the prophet lies on his left side for 390 days and then on his right side for 40 days!) – not to mention his famous vision of the throne of God, with its 'wheels within wheels' and 'their rims full of eyes' (Ezekiel 1)!

It was in 1877 that the hypothesis of Ezekiel's mental illness was first clearly articulated, by August Klostermann, who spoke of 'catalepsy'.[8] The classic presentation of the theory is found in a famous article of 1946 by Broome.[9] This purported to be a real case-study; the diagnosis included the words 'catatonia', 'paranoia', 'psychosis' and 'schizophrenia'. In such ways were explained Ezekiel's dumbness, his withdrawal and the other strange features of his behaviour. Lest it be imagined that this is a line of enquiry and interpretation which has attracted only those who are themselves inclined to eccentricity, it should be noted that even Hermann Gunkel, one of the greatest biblical scholars of modern times and generally a model of judgement, resorted to explanations such as nervous derangement or an irrepressible unconscious when discussing features of the book of Ezekiel.[10] The most influential rebuttal of Broome's developed theory is found in a chapter of C. G. Howie's book of 1950.[11] Howie argued that adequate explanations can be given for each of the odd features of Ezekiel's reported behaviour, explanations which accommodate him within the (in any case broad) range of the 'normal'. For Howie, Ezekiel was a mystic, but not a madman. In Germany, Jaspers' study of 1947 – independent of both Broome and Howie – offered a judicious reflection on all these questions, highlighting some important questions of method.[12]

Since the 1950s, the general consensus has been that the theory of Ezekiel's mental illness was a false trail in interpretation, which was rightly abandoned. It is rather surprising, therefore, that in a new, major book, David Joel Halperin has not only revived the hypothesis, but has done so at greater length and in more thoroughgoing fashion than ever before. The book is called *Seeking Ezekiel: Text and Psychology*.[13] Halperin attempts to use the text of the book of Ezekiel as the basis for nothing less than the psychoanalysis of the man Ezekiel, and gives an account of the whole text in these terms. He postulates a person dominated by a pathological dread and loathing of female sexuality. Close attention is given to the vivid, some would say pornographic, presentations of Israel as woman in chapters 16 and 23, and to Ezekiel's failure to mourn his wife's death in chapter 24. And a central place is given to the strange episode in Ezekiel 8.7–12, in which the prophet digs a hole through a wall and enters a chamber in which are portrayed all kinds of loathsome beasts. It is not surprising to learn that this is interpreted as an image for sexual intercourse!

It must be stressed that, although what has been reported may sound somewhat bizarre, Halperin's book is an important one from a distinguished scholar (previously best known for his work on the place of Ezekiel's 'chariot' vision in Jewish tradition). It is based on a close reading of and detailed discussion of the Hebrew text. Indeed, Halperin is reluctant ever to propose textual emendations and he resists proposals to reorder the text or to stratify it into 'primary' or 'secondary' levels. The fact that Halperin is not a professional psychologist or psychoanalyst (but rather a scholar of biblical and Jewish studies) should not be regarded as a fatal criticism of his project. He is widely read and well-informed in these fields, and it is vital for the health of biblical studies that such bridges between disciplines are kept open, indeed that biblical studies be conducted in the public domain in this way.

However, there is much about the scope and manner of Halperin's treatment which calls for serious criticism. I wish to highlight two main issues, of which the first is Halperin's marked tendency to go beyond the evidence of the text of the book of Ezekiel. The scant personal details found in this ancient text are an insufficient basis for a project as bold as a psychoanalysis. Many people are, of course, sceptical about the viability of the psychoanalysis even of a modern contemporary, with hundreds of hours of two-way conversation. Whether such scepticism is justified or not, how much more uncertain must be the psychoanalysis of an ancient figure, of whom no questions can be asked? And yet Halperin attempts to paint a very detailed picture of Ezekiel's inner life, particularly in relation to his sexuality, venturing far beyond what, on any showing, the available data could justify.

One of the distinctive, and at least superficially rather promising, features of Halperin's presentation is his self-critical awareness that difficult questions of method are raised by his approach. Having acknowledged these issues, Halperin proceeds, as it were, in the face of them, arguing that his approach will nonetheless be vindicated if it yields more satisfactory answers to numerous long-debated problems of text and interpretation than do alternative approaches. Since Halperin himself in this way invites judgement on the basis of how much new light his psychoanalytical reading sheds on old problems of interpretation, it seems fair to take an example of a long-discussed critical problem presented by Ezekiel, namely why the prophet's dumbness ends when the news reaches him of the fall of the Jerusalem Temple (Ezek 24.27; 33.22). Halperin explains this on the basis of the theory that the city and Temple represent the feminine. God, as 'tyrannical parent', has, through the catastrophe of 587 BCE, destroyed these symbols of the feminine, thereby apparently vindicating Ezekiel's negative feelings towards the feminine and relieving him of the acute guilt feelings which had caused his dumbness. Whilst it is not possible here to explore this issue in detail, it must be said that Halperin's interpretation (typical of his tendency to go beyond the available evidence) seems a particularly forced one, in no way superior to the established range of more straightforward explanations. On Halperin's own 'exegetical gain' test, he would seem, then, in this case at least, to have failed.[14]

The second major criticism may be summarized in terms of Halperin's tendency to take psychological issues in isolation from other important perspectives. I wish to highlight three respects, sociological, literary and theological, in which essential dimensions of the text of Ezekiel are overlooked by him. Two of these (involving sociological and literary perspectives) represent important ways in which features of public discourse other than psychology have impinged creatively on biblical studies of late.

Recent years have seen much fruitful application of the insights of sociology in biblical studies.[15] More specifically, a good deal has been learned about the social roles performed by prophets in ancient Israel, and the ways in which they interacted with society as a whole.[16] In contrast to this, Halperin's reading is (in spite of his own disclaimers[17]) a strongly individualizing one, which takes Ezekiel in isolation from his context and fails to do justice to the growing recognition of the importance of the social dimension of Israelite prophecy.

Earlier reference was made to the upsurge of literary perspectives in biblical studies. This is another area of insight upon which Halperin fails to draw. Halperin is, perhaps surprisingly, very 'literalistic' in his treatment of the text, which is used with much confidence as a historical source for Ezekiel's life, both outer and inner. His study is lacking in any real sense that the book of Ezekiel is a work of literature. However, it is now increasingly recognized that the books of the prophets are by no means straightforward reports by the prophets of their personal experiences. There are clear indications that they have been 'worked on' in a complex redactional process, and that they are sophisticated literary texts.[18] The characterization of Ezekiel in the book which bears his name is to be read with sensitivity to this. The first-person 'I' narrative style of the book can be paralleled in numerous Ancient Near Eastern texts which are certainly not autobiographies.[19] One must be on the look out for literary motifs and aware of the place of the book of Ezekiel in developing Israelite tradition. The presentation of Ezekiel must be seen as echoing certain features of the so-called 'primitive' prophets of old, such as Elisha.[20] The images of women must be read in the light of earlier presentations, in Isaiah and especially in Hosea. The bizarre visions which characterize the book of Ezekiel must be seen in the context of a developing tradition of imagery, which would later play a significant part in shaping the idioms of apocalyptic literature.

A further deficiency in Halperin's approach is his lack of a theological perspective. He is quite frank about this – for example, the wrath of God is to be interpreted reductionistically as a projection of Ezekiel's own rage.[21] For someone who claims to be handling the literature on its own terms, as Halperin does, this lack of theological perspective is surely a serious shortcoming. For example, much is made of Ezekiel's failure to mourn his wife, as recounted in chapter 24. But it is vital to see that a theological point is being made in the paralleling of the wife's death with the fall of the Jerusalem Temple. The latter tragedy is richly deserved by Israel, and the refusal to allow proper mourning is to be seen as compounding the punishment of sin. None of this is dealt with adequately by Halperin. Indeed, here, in the reductionistic failure to engage with the theological dimension of texts which are, after all, primarily theological, we see one of the major problems attending much psychological reading of the Bible.

Do these criticisms amount to a calling into question of all attempts to bring the insights of psychology to bear on biblical studies? By no means. Used judiciously and applied self-critically, psychological insights can shed much light on ancient texts. There are certainly pitfalls to be avoided, but the real gains are many. With regard to Ezekiel, reference has already been made to the important work of Julie Galambush, which combines psychological insights with feminist criticism and also more traditional historical-critical scholarship – an excellent example of a treatment of Ezekiel learning from many different features of 'public discourse'.[22] Turning to other biblical books, I have attempted elsewhere to demonstrate that modern studies of the psychology of loss and bereavement can help us understand the lament literature of the Hebrew Bible, notably the book of Lamentations.[23] The New Testament has certainly not escaped interpretation from a psychological perspective; here the work of Gerd Theissen has been especially important.[24] Another fascinating – and rather different – area of study is into the very process of modern reading of ancient texts: psychological awareness can play a valuable part in helping one understand some of the dynamics at work in interpretation.[25]

We have emphasized that the Bible is inevitably read in the light of the broad intellectual context of its readers. Since psychological insights play an important part in that context for most modern people, it is desirable that their role and contribution should be acknowledged and critically examined. Psychological readings can do much to open up ways in which the myths and symbols of the Bible may function afresh in our time. But it is only if such work is done with restraint and in a genuinely self-critical spirit that this potentially rich line of enquiry will make its proper contribution. Moreover, as we have seen, it is important to avoid the expectation that any one approach will answer all our questions. Psychological insights taken in isolation provide insufficient tools for the multifaceted task of interpretation of a biblical text, and so it is hardly surprising that Halperin's failure to complement psychological enquiry with a range of sociological, literary and theological questions seriously vitiates his enterprise.

Much reference has been made here to the impact of modernity. But many today are exploring what it may mean to live in a *postmodern* situation.[26] By this is meant, among many other things, a situation in which the preoccupation with historical questions which once dominated the reading of texts has retreated to the point where readers are unrestricted in the meanings that they can legitimately find in a text (there are obvious, though often complex, points of contact between this phenomenon and many of those new approaches in biblical studies which put a strong emphasis on the situation and response of the reader). Within a postmodern context, psychological perspectives can bring much to a text like Ezekiel. This is all very different from Halperin's approach, however; his stance could be described as a characteristically 'modernist' one, with its concern to establish the facts about the historical figure Ezekiel. Because that is Halperin's acknowledged aim, it is quite right that he should be criticized when he does not carry it through with appropriate caution. In a postmodernist setting, however, matters are quite other, for the need for caution about going beyond the historical evidence of the text can be forgotten. The reader is not constrained by any need to be faithful to the original meaning of the text, even if this could with confidence be recovered. Instead, psychological insights can, in a lively and uninhibited way, enrich the reader's playful, imaginative exploration of the text – and of course Ezekiel is a text which gives plenty of food for thought![27] Part of the attraction of postmodernism lies in its very open-endedness, the apparently infinite range of perspectives which can feed the imagination in the process of reading; and so I would contend that, whilst psychological insights may have a particularly rich contribution to make in this context, a reading informed only by psychological perspectives will, here too, prove to be an excessively narrow one. Rather, the richer and more varied the fields of association brought to a text the better: social as well as individual; poetic as well as prosaic; secular as well as religious; 'popular' as well as classical.[28]

In conclusion, there can be no denying that a serious question mark stands against the role of the Bible in our time, both within society at large and within the Church. Doubts about its continued capacity to function as a publicly acknowledged point of reference are to be taken with full seriousness. But the situation is a complex one, with traffic both ways. New modes in which the Bible can function are emerging, just as others are retreating. This makes for a very exciting situation. It is tempting to fall into a nostalgia which hankers after old situations in which the Bible had a clearly acknowledged place; but such longing for old treasures can blind one to new, if unexpected, gifts (whether they come in the form of literary approaches, psychological readings or postmodernism). We are challenged to be ready to let go of the old, so as to be free to be surprised and delighted by the new. To end, as we began, with Freddie Mercury and Queen: 'The Show Must Go On . . .'

Notes

1. On some of the other issues raised in connection with relativism, see D. E. Nineham, *The Use and Abuse of the Bible: A Study of the Bible in a Period of Rapid Cultural Change* (London: Macmillan, 1976); and, more recently, his *Christianity Mediaeval and Modern* (London: SCM Press, 1993).
2. For an accessible introduction to many of the newer approaches, see R. J. Coggins, *Introducing the Old Testament* (Oxford: Oxford University Press, 1990).
3. See further, P. M. Joyce, 'First among equals? The historical-critical approach in the marketplace of methods' in Stanley E. Porter, Paul M. Joyce and David E. Orton (eds), *Crossing the Boundaries: Essays in Biblical Interpretation in Honour of Professor Michael D. Goulder* (Leiden: E. J. Brill, 1994).
4. N. Frye, *The Great Code: The Bible and Literature* (London, etc.: Routledge and Kegan Paul, 1982); R. Alter and F. Kermode (eds), *The Literary Guide to the Bible* (London: Collins, 1987); G. Josipovici, *The Book of God: A Response to the Bible* (New Haven and London: Yale University Press, 1988).
5. Cf. A. Berlin, *Poetics and Interpretation of Biblical Narrative* (Bible and Literature Series 9; Sheffield: Almond Press, 1983); H. C. Brichto, *Toward a Grammar of Biblical Poetics:*

Tales of the Prophets (New York/Oxford: Oxford University Press, 1992); D. M. Gunn and D. N. Fewell, *Narrative in the Hebrew Bible* (Oxford Bible Series; Oxford: Oxford University Press, 1993).
6. See, for example, W. G. Jeanrond, *Theological Hermeneutics: Development and Significance* (Basingstoke: Macmillan, 1991); A. C. Thiselton, *New Horizons in Hermeneutics* (London: HarperCollins, 1992).
7. Cf. J. Barr, *Fundamentalism* (London: SCM Press, 1977).
8. A. Klostermann, 'Ezechiel: Ein Beitrag zu besserer Würdigung seiner Person und seiner Schrift', *Theologische Studien und Kritiken* 50 (1877), pp. 391–439.
9. E. C. Broome, 'Ezekiel's abnormal personality', *Journal of Biblical Literature* 65 (1946), pp. 277–92.
10. Cf. H. Gunkel, 'Israelite prophecy from the time of Amos' in J. Pelikan (ed.), *Twentieth Century Theology in the Making* (New York: Harper and Row, 1969), vol. 1, pp. 48–75.
11. C. G. Howie, *The Date and Composition of Ezekiel* (Journal of Biblical Literature Monograph Series 4; Philadelphia: Journal of Biblical Literature, 1950), pp. 69–84.
12. K. Jaspers, 'Der Prophet Ezechiel: Eine pathographische Studie', *Arbeiten zur Psychiatrie, Neurologie und ihren Grenzgebieten. Festschrift K. Schneider* (Heidelberg, 1947), pp. 77–85.
13. D. J. Halperin, *Seeking Ezekiel: Text and Psychology* (University Park, PA: Pennsylvania University Press, 1993).
14. The observation that the city and the Temple are represented in feminine terms is not in itself, of course, untrue; what is problematic is what Halperin goes on to do with this insight. For a more judicious handling of this theme see the work of Julie Galambush: J. Galambush, *Jerusalem in the Book of Ezekiel: The City as Yahweh's Wife* (SBL Dissertation Series 130; Atlanta, GA: Scholars Press, 1992).
15. Cf. A. D. H. Mayes, *The Old Testament in Sociological Perspective* (London: Marshall Pickering, 1989); R. R. Wilson, *Sociological Approaches to the Old Testament* (Philadelphia: Fortress Press, 1984).
16. E.g. R. R. Wilson, *Prophecy and Society in Ancient Israel* (Philadelphia: Fortress Press, 1980); D. L. Petersen, *The Roles of Israel's Prophets* (Journal for the Study of the Old Testament Supplement Series 17; Sheffield: JSOT Press, 1981).
17. Halperin, op. cit., pp. 220–1.
18. Cf. T. Collins, *The Mantle of Elijah: The Reduction Criticism of the Prophetical Books* (The Biblical Seminar 20; Sheffield: JSOT Press, 1993).
19. E.g. from Mesopotamia, the epic of Gilgamesh; and, from Egypt, the story of Sinuhe.
20. Cf. K. W. Carley, *Ezekiel Among the Prophets: A Study of Ezekiel's Place in Prophetic Tradition* (Studies in Biblical Theology, second series 31; London: SCM Press, 1975).
21. Halperin, op. cit., p. 4.
22. Galambush, op. cit.
23. P. M. Joyce, 'Lamentations and the grief process: a psychological reading', *Biblical Interpretation* 1, 3 (1993), pp. 304–20.
24. G. Theissen, *Psychological Aspects of Pauline Theology* (Edinburgh: T. & T. Clark, 1987).
25. For a useful survey of 'Psychological interpretation', see the article of that name by D. K. Miell in R. J. Coggins and J. L. Houlden (eds), *A Dictionary of Biblical Interpretation* (London: SCM Press/Philadelphia: Trinity Press International, 1990), pp. 571–2.
26. Cf. Madan Sarup, *An Introductory Guide to Post-Structuralism and Postmodernism* (2nd edn, New York, London, etc.: Harvester Wheatsheaf, 1993). Participation in a shared

conversation with non-theologians who are involved in the postmodernist movement is another respect in which many biblical scholars are these days conducting their work within a much broader cultural context than hitherto.

27. The present writer, whilst open to the gifts and challenges of postmodernism, wishes in fact to retain a 'place of honour' for historical concerns in the reading of texts. Cf. P. M. Joyce, 'First among equals?', op. cit.

28. There is room here only to hint at the possibilities presented for biblical studies through a dialogue with postmodernism. See further W. Brueggemann, *The Bible and Postmodern Imagination: Texts Under Negotiation* (London: SCM Press, 1993).

6
Religious language after the Holocaust

Isabel Wollaston

> What shall I liken to thee, what shall I equal to thee that I may comfort thee? For thy breach is great like the sea; who can heal thee? (Lam 2.13)

This verse encapsulates the theme that I wish to explore: continuity and discontinuity in language (religious or otherwise) after the Holocaust. This text bears witness to continuity in that it is from the book of Lamentations. The book is recited in its entirety on Tisha Be'Av, the day in the Jewish calendar set aside to remember the destruction of the first and second Temples. In addition, Lamentations provides the model for *kinot* (dirges) written to commemorate the victims of subsequent disasters. These *kinot* are woven into the liturgy of Tisha Be'Av, thus providing continuity in the response to catastrophe down the ages. It therefore comes as no surprise to find Orthodox writers citing this verse as proof that the Holocaust poses no *new* theological challenge: the tradition provides resources now, just as it has in the past.[1] Yet we find the same verse cited in support of the claim that the Holocaust marks a radical break with tradition, resulting in a breach that cannot be healed.[2] My proposal is that this difference in interpretation indicates the possibility of a third option: the fact that this verse *can* be employed in both of these ways suggests that a response to the Holocaust needs to allow for the possibility – and legitimacy – of *both* continuity and discontinuity, while avoiding the privileging of either.

Before considering the specific question of religious language, it is necessary to establish whether we can, in fact, speak about the Holocaust *per se*. The belief that the Holocaust is incomprehensible and/or incommunicable underlies much that is written on the subject, and is central to the argument that it is a breach that cannot be healed. It is by now almost standard practice to insist that the Holocaust is beyond speech. This conviction is shared by victims, survivors and critics. Chaim Kaplan lamented 'my powers are insufficient to record all that is worthy of being written'.[3] The survivor Elie Wiesel has probably done as much as anyone in establishing this view:

> Ask any survivor, he will tell you, he who has not lived through the event will never know it. And he who went through it, will not reveal it – not really, not entirely. Between his memory and its reflection there is a wall – and it cannot be pierced. The past belongs to the dead, and the survivor does not recognize himself in the words linking him to them.[4]

A similar point was made by Primo Levi. He was adamant that the 'true story' could not be told because the testimony of the survivors was, at best, 'a discourse on "behalf of third parties", the story of things seen close by, not experienced personally'. The 'true story' was that of the 'drowned', the *Muselmänner*, who, by definition, had no story.[5] What precisely is being said here by Levi and Wiesel? It is obvious that they are not claiming that it is literally impossible to speak about the event(s). For, as has often been noted, it is ironic that there should be 'so much talk about silence'.[6] Are these writers trying to express an emotional truth, to convey a sense of awe and hopelessness in the face of such destruction? Yes, but it is also more than that. Levi and Wiesel strive to communicate their sense of being trapped in a paradoxical situation: on the one hand, the witness is compelled to speak on behalf of the dead; on the other hand, the witness is convinced that it is impossible to communicate all that needs to be said.

Such a paradox has its roots in the nature of the Holocaust itself. The Nazis' intention was that the Holocaust would be an 'event without a witness': no trace would be left of the destruction of the Jews.[7] If the Holocaust had been completely – as opposed to only partially – successful, the Jews would now be remembered solely on the Nazis' terms, as in the planned Jewish museum in Prague. Thus, from the victims' perspective, bearing witness to their fate was 'an act of war against fascism'.[8] They were determined that their testimony would survive, even if they themselves did not. The problem confronting the survivor stems from the extent to which the Holocaust *was* successful: whereas the victims were unaware of the full scale of the destruction, the survivors have no such illusions. In many instances, there were only one or two survivors out of an entire community:

> as family, as friends are killed, each becomes the last Jew, the only survivor: 'And I alone have survived to tell thee.'[9]

In the case of Eastern Europe, an entire religious culture was effectively wiped out. Whereas pre-war Poland was arguably the spiritual centre of world Jewry, post-war Poland is often spoken of as a graveyard. In effect, the Holocaust marks the amputation of what had been one of world Jewry's most vital 'limbs'.[10] The survivors – and the few writings left behind by the victims – become the only trace of what was destroyed. The irony of this is that – of necessity – when the fate of the Jews is remembered in Holocaust museums, it is primarily through the evidence left behind by the Nazis rather than their victims.[11]

When the survivor does bear witness, it is as much in an attempt to 'put the pages of the book back together', to (re-)establish some semblance of continuity with the past from which they were severed so abruptly, as to communicate their experience to those who were not there. In bearing witness to the Holocaust, the survivor is often struggling with a sense of having 'outlived' his or her own death:

> for the witnesses, the Holocaust is at once a lived and a 'died' event: the paradox of how one survives a died event is one of the most urgent (if unobtrusive) topics of their testimonies.[12]

As we shall see, one of the dilemmas confronting those attempting to articulate religious responses to the Holocaust is whether it is possible to speak of redemption in relation to a 'died' event.

Thus, references to the incommunicability of the Holocaust serve to indicate the problematic nature of discourse in this context. Two primary strategies are employed in response. The first aims to communicate the impossibility of communication. In his introduction to Lyotard's *Heidegger and 'the jews'*, David Carroll notes that the phrase 'let's not talk about that' (or variations upon it) serves as a constant refrain throughout Claude Lanzmann's film *Shoah*. Indeed, Lanzmann's persistence in forcing his interviewees to talk about 'that' – in spite of their obvious reluctance – proved to be one of the most controversial elements in the film.[13] Carroll observes that the plea not to talk about a subject provides a way of beginning to talk about that subject by, at the very least, indicating the impossibility of talking about 'that'.[14] A similar point is made by Lyotard, when he suggests that:

> the silence surrounding the phrase 'Auschwitz was the extermination camp' is . . . a sign that something remains to be phrased, which is not, something which is not determined.[15]

In other words, the inability, or refusal, to speak about certain things indicates that there is something more that 'remains to be phrased', and that what remains exceeds that which has been said (a strategy not unfamiliar from negative theology). By focusing solely on details, or upon stories that may appear to be tangential, it is possible to indicate something of the nature of that which is not being said. By describing the 'how', it is possible to indicate factors that might have a bearing on the 'why'.[16]

A second, and arguably more traditional, response is that of the lament. It is possible to argue that Jewish responses to catastrophe constitute a lamentation tradition.[17] Jewish self-understanding in the light of disaster is refracted through a series of key texts and archetypes (Genesis 22, Job, Lamentations, the woman and her seven sons, the Ten Martyrs, and so on). Lamentation takes the form of a three-way dialogue between the writer, the covenantal people and God: although, often, the lament is addressed by the writer(s), on behalf of the people, to a silent or absent God. Alan Mintz suggests that Lamentations itself can be read as a record of humanity's struggle to speak in the face of God's silence.[18] Rather than breaking down, a secular version of the lamentation tradition emerged in the modern period. These 'secular' laments employ traditional archetypes and literary forms, but with the purpose of subverting them, in order to highlight their inadequacy when confronted by more recent catastrophes. Examples of this latter approach are Chaim Nachman Bialik's 'In the City of the Slaughter' (written in response to the Kishinev pogrom of 1903) and Yitzhak Katzenelson's 'Song of the Slaughtered Jewish People' (written during the Holocaust). David Roskies suggests that the lamentation tradition allows for two possible responses: 'literal recall' (as in the modelling of *kinot* on the book of Lamentations), or 'sacred parody', 'imitating the breach of God's promise in the parody of scripture' (as in Bialik and Katzenelson's subversion of the traditional lament).[19] While 'literal recall' is more obviously a means of keeping faith, so too is 'sacred parody':

> by incorporating the anger, even the blasphemy, into the normative response to catastrophe, the language of sacred parody remains contained yet infinitely expandable; scriptural and liturgical texts can be appropriated while registering the enormity of the violation of central precepts.[20]

However, the question then arises as to whether traditional religious vocabulary is, in fact, 'infinitely expandable'. Up to what point can 'sacred parody' remain 'contained'? When does it mark a break with, or the collapse of, traditional responses to catastrophe? Sidra Ezrahi suggests that 'sacred parody' requires a precarious balancing act:

> For those who remain within the parameters of the tradition, the attempt to recreate the Holocaust in terms of its collective legacy is accompanied

> by the risk of exposing the ruptures, the discontinuities, and the cracks in the most fundamental codes of Jewish faith and conduct.[21]

In many ways, the question of religious language after the Holocaust is similar to that posed in relation to the lamentation tradition: does the attempt to speak of God after the Holocaust serve only to expose 'the ruptures, the discontinuities, and the cracks'? Irving Greenberg suggests that it does. He asks whether 'even those who believe after such an event dare talk about God who loves and cares, without making a mockery of those who suffered'. For Greenberg, the 'testimony of the six million is so strong that it all but irretrievably closes out religious language'. After the Holocaust, the most – and maybe the only – credible religious testimony is a commitment to the restoration of the human as the image of God.[22] Yet, in contrast, many Orthodox thinkers insist that nothing has changed: it is as possible to talk about God now as it was before; the Holocaust changes nothing. How are we to reconcile these two positions? Greenberg's reference to 'the testimony of the six million' suggests one possible response. It is now commonplace to insist that it is possible to pray *after* Auschwitz only because prayer was possible – at least for some – *in* Auschwitz. A spectrum of responses concerning belief is to be found in the testimony of those who experienced the Holocaust. As a consequence, it is often suggested that any contemporary response is 'authentic' to the extent that it was possible then. Such a view is given extreme form by Elie Wiesel: 'I never speak of God now. I rather speak of men who believed in God or men who disbelieved in God.'[23]

A more moderate, but potentially more controversial, position is that of Eliezer Berkovits. He argues that while those who were in the camps were in the position of Job, those who come after are in the position of 'Job's brother'. As a result, 'those of us who were not there must, before anything else, heed the responses of those who were there'.[24] In Berkovits' view, those who were there responded in two ways, either by:

> pious submission . . . as a manifestation of the Divine will . . . [or] the more frequent attitude of the one who questions and doubts, a position that may ultimately lead to outright rebellion against the very idea of a beneficent providence.[25]

Today, 'Job's brother', if he wishes to be true to both of these responses, 'reasons with God in believing rebellion and rebellious belief'.[26] However, is it possible to maintain this tension, without privileging one response at the expense of the other? In the case of Berkovits, it would appear that it is not. Despite the fact that he emphasizes the need for 'Job's brother' to remain true to both responses, he draws a distinction between the two: while 'the faith affirmed was superhuman', the loss of faith was 'human'.[27] Berkovits then elaborates. He refers to the 'authentic Jew' who 'wanted to survive like anyone else, but not at any cost; not at the cost of betraying the meaning of his own life'.[28] By introducing a category as loaded as 'authenticity', he inevitably implies that some Jewish responses were 'inauthentic'. On what grounds can such a judgement be made?

A similar dilemma is apparent in the work of Emil Fackenheim. Throughout his work, he stresses that the Holocaust is:

> an event that called into question all things – God, man, the ancient revelation and the modern secular self-confidence, philosophic thought, and indeed thought of any kind.[29]

The negative effects of the Holocaust are encapsulated in the figure of the *Muselmann*. Yet, at the same time, Fackenheim is adamant that *tikkun* (mending) is possible. The basis for such *tikkun* lies in the fact that, during the Holocaust, there were those who resisted the Nazi logic of destruction and dehumanization. This resistance could take numerous forms: the actions of the Ghetto fighters and partisans, the victims' determination to bear witness, the piety of the *haredim*, the daily struggle to survive and so on. Belief, and indeed hope, are only possible now because they were possible then – typified by resistance to the Nazis in all its forms. However, is Fackenheim not also privileging one response, at the expense of others? What has happened to the rupture generated by the 'testimony' of the *Muselmänner*? Is this negative witness included in the 'mending'?

The determination of both Berkovits and Fackenheim not only to salvage something from the wreckage, but also to find something positive that will serve as inspiration for those who come after, is laudable. Yet, in spite of their determination to be true to the full spectrum of response, each ultimately privileges those of affirmation over those of negation. Such privileging is perhaps inevitable. However, it runs counter to the principle of respect for the multiplicity of responses to the Holocaust: 'the logic of privilege necessarily implies that something else is excluded or made secondary.'[30] As a counterbalance to Berkovits and Fackenheim, it is necessary that 'the testimony of radical negation' be both recognized and heard. One of the consequences of hearing such testimony is that it 'challenges the credibility of redemptive thinking'.[31] At the same time, hearing the testimony of radical negation should not blind us to the testimony of affirmation highlighted by Berkovits, Fackenheim and others. If listening to the testimony of those who were there is a prerequisite for any response to the Holocaust, then, in one sense, those who argue that nothing has changed and those who argue that everything has changed are both correct, for both of these responses are found among those who were there.

Perhaps this is why Wiesel prefers to speak of 'men who believed in God or men who disbelieved in God', rather than to speak of God directly. By employing the model of testimony, he avoids privileging any one response, by incorporating them all. In this way, it is possible to maintain the ambiguities and unresolved tensions between the various responses. For Wiesel, the scope of the disaster was such that each individual response must be respected:

> my only answer is that I would not like to see any point of view prevail over the others. On the contrary, there must remain an open question, a conflict.[32]

The question that then arises is whether such openness is compatible with the enterprise of theology. Perhaps it is significant that Wiesel is vehemently opposed to any such enterprise.

Notes

1. See, for example, Rabbi Isaac Swift, 'Mourning and consolation' in Bernhard H. Rosenberg (ed.), *Theological and Halakhic Responses to the Holocaust* (Hoboken, NJ: KTAV, 1992), pp. 3–8 (p. 6).
2. See, for example, Susan Shapiro, 'For thy breach is great like the sea, who can heal thee?', *Religious Studies Review* 13.3 (1987), pp. 210–13.
3. Chaim Kaplan (trans. and ed. A. I. Katsh), *Scroll of Agony: The Warsaw Ghetto Diary of Chaim A. Kaplan* (London: Hamish Hamilton, 1966), p. 313 (entry for 31 July 1942).
4. Elie Wiesel, 'Art and culture after the Holocaust' in Eva Fleischner (ed.), *Auschwitz: Beginning of a New Era?* (New York: KTAV, 1977), pp. 403–15 (p. 405).
5. See Primo Levi, *The Drowned and the Saved* (Michael Joseph, 1988), pp. 62–4, and *If This Is a Man* (Abacus, 1987), pp. 94–6.
6. Yael Feldman, 'Whose story is it anyway?' in Saul Friedlander (ed.), *Probing the Limits of Representation: Nazism and the 'Final Solution'* (Cambridge, MA: Harvard University Press, 1992) pp. 223–39 (p. 228).
7. Shoshana Felman, 'Film as witness' in Geoffrey Hartman (ed.), *Holocaust Remembrance* (Oxford: Basil Blackwell, 1994), pp. 90–103 (p. 96); and Shoshana Felman and Dori Laub, *Testimony: Crises of Witnessing in Literature, Psychoanalysis, and History* (Routledge, 1992), pp. 75–92, 204–83. See also Jean François Lyotard's comment:

> it had to be the perfect crime, one would plead not guilty, certain of the lack of proofs. This is a politics of absolute forgetting, forgotten.

(Heidegger and 'the jews' (Minneapolis: University of Minneapolis, 1990), p. 25).
8. Levi, *The Drowned and the Saved*, p. 7.
9. Hartman (ed.), op. cit., p. 4.
10. For example, Stanislaw Krajewski comments:

> Jews see Poland as a forsaken place where Jewish culture flourished a long time ago, then it got worse and worse, it all ended in tragedy, and there is now only a painful absence.

(in Andrzej Bryk, 'Poland and the memory of the Holocaust', *Partisan Review* 57.2 (1990), pp. 228–38 (p. 233)). For a more detailed discussion of the impact of the Holocaust upon Poland's Jews, see Chimen Abramsky, Maciej Jachimczyk and Antony Polonsky (eds), *The Jews in Poland* (Oxford: Basil Blackwell, 1986) pp. 147–208; Iwona Irwin-Zarecka, *Neutralizing Memory: The Jew in Contemporary Poland* (New Brunswick: Transaction Publishers, 1989); Antony Polonsky (ed.), *My Brother's Keeper? Recent Polish Debates on the Holocaust* (Routledge, 1990), pp. 1–33, 98–109, 161–232; James E. Young, *The Texture of Memory: Holocaust Memorials and Their Meaning* (New Haven: Yale University Press, 1993), pp. 113–208, particularly pp. 185–208.

11. This point has been made with reference to both Auschwitz and the recently opened United States Holocaust Memorial Museum (USHMM) in Washington, DC. See Young, op. cit., pp. 132–3, 342–7. With reference to the USHMM, it is perhaps significant that many commentators refer to the impact of the Tower of Faces, a collection of more than 1,000 photographs, taken between 1900 and 1941, of the inhabitants of the Jewish *shtetl* Ejszyszki in Lithuania. The inhabitants were shot on 25–26 September 1941. In the Museum, these photographs form 'a tower representing the Jewish lives that were and are no longer', so that 'through the fate of one community we learn the fate of others'. See Michael Berenbaum, *The World Must Know: The History of the Holocaust As Told in the United States Holocaust Memorial Museum* (Boston: Little, Brown and Company, 1993); Helen Belitsky, 'Memory and accidental tourists', *Hadassah* 74.8 (1993), pp. 26–30; Brendan Gill, 'The Holocaust Museum: an unquiet sanctuary', *New Yorker* (19 April 1993), pp. 107–9; Geordie Gregg, 'From here to eternity', *Sunday Times* (9 May 1993); Charles Krauthammer, 'Holocaust Museum: where infamy achieves immortality', *Washington Post* (23 April 1993); Leon Wieseltier, 'After memory', *New Republic* (2 May 1993), pp. 14–26; George Will, 'Telling their truth', *Baltimore Sun* (22 April 1993).

12. Lawrence Langer, *Holocaust Testimonies: The Ruins of Memory* (New Haven: Yale University Press, 1991), pp. 69, 149. See also Langer, 'Remembering survival' in Hartman (ed.), op. cit., pp. 70–80.

13. The most controversial example is Lanzmann's persistence in questioning Abraham Bomba, see *Shoah: An Oral History of the Holocaust* (New York: Pantheon, 1985), pp. 111–17:

> *Bomba*: I can't. It's too horrible. Please.
> *Lanzmann*: We have to do it. You know it.
> *Bomba*: I won't be able to do it.
> *Lanzmann*: You have to do it. I know it's very hard. I know and I apologize.
> *Bomba*: Don't make me go on please.
> *Lanzmann*: Please. We must go on.
> *Bomba*: I told you today it's going to be very hard. (p. 117)

14. David Carroll, 'The memory of the devastation and the responsibilities of thought: "And let's not talk about that"' in Lyotard, op. cit., pp. vii–xxix. He is referring to a conversation between Lanzmann and Michael Podchlebnik about Simon Srebnik (Srebnik and Podchlebnik were the only two survivors of Chelmno):

> *Lanzmann*: What died in him in Chelmno?
> *Podchlebnik*: Everything died. But he's only human, and he wants to live. So he must forget. He thanks God for what remains, and that he can forget. And let's not talk about that.

Lanzmann: Does he think it's good to talk about it?
Podchlebnik: For me it's not good.
Lanzmann: Then why is he talking about it?
Podchlebnik: Because you're insisting on it. (p. 7)

This passage is also cited and analysed by Shoshana Felman. See Felman and Laub, op. cit., pp. 224–5.

15. Jean François Lyotard, *The Differend: Phrases in Dispute* (Manchester University Press, 1988), pp. 56–7. On the theme of silence and the limits of representation in relation to the Holocaust, see also Maurice Blanchot, *The Writing of the Disaster* (Lincoln: University of Nebraska Press, 1986); Friedlander (ed.), op. cit., pp. 3–4; Michael Lustigman, *Kindness of Truth and the Art of Reading Ashes* (New York: Peter Lang, 1988); George Steiner, 'The long life of metaphor: an approach to the *Shoah*', *Encounter* (February 1987).

16. The strategy of describing the 'how' rather than the 'why' underpins the permanent exhibition at the USHMM. See the introduction by the Director of the Museum to Berenbaum, op. cit. This strategy is also employed throughout Lanzmann's *Shoah*. The methodology of the film is summed up by the historian Raul Hilberg:

> In all of my work I have never begun by asking the big questions, because I was afraid that I would come up with small answers; and I have preferred to address these things which are minutiae or details in order that I might then be able to put together in a gestalt a picture which, if not an explanation, is at least a description, a more full description, of what transpired. (*Shoah*, p. 70)

Wiesel focuses upon the apparently tangential in order to highlight what is *not* being said:

> The tales that I tell are never the ones that I would like to tell, or ought to tell.

(*From the Kingdom of Memory* (New York: Summit Books, 1990), p. 143).

17. For a fuller discussion of the lamentation tradition as a response to catastrophe, see Sidra Dekoven Ezrahi, *By Words Alone: The Holocaust in Literature* (Chicago: University of Chicago Press, 1980), pp. 96–148; Ezrahi, 'Considering the Apocalypse' in Berel Lang (ed.), *Writing and the Holocaust* (New York: Holmes and Meier, 1988), pp. 137–53; Alan Mintz, *Hurban: Responses to Catastrophe in Hebrew Literature* (New York: Columbia University Press, 1984); David Roskies, *Against the Apocalypse: Responses to Catastrophe in Modern Jewish Thought* (Cambridge: Harvard University Press, 1984); Roskies, *The Literature of Destruction* (Philadelphia: Jewish Publication Society of America, 1989); Roskies, 'The library of catastrophe' in Hartman (ed.), op. cit., pp. 33–41; Yosef Hayim Yerushalmi, *Zakhor: Jewish History and Jewish Memory* (New York: Schocken, 1989).

18. Alan Mintz, 'The rhetoric of Lamentations and the representation of catastrophe', *Prooftexts* 2 (1982), pp. 1–17.

19. Roskies, *Against the Apocalypse*, pp. 17, 20.

20. Ezrahi, 'Considering the Apocalypse', p. 141.

21. Ezrahi, *By Words Alone*, p. 148.

22. Irving Greenberg, 'Cloud of smoke, pillar of fire: Judaism, Christianity, and modernity after the Holocaust' in Fleischner (ed.), op. cit., pp. 7–55. See also Greenberg, 'Judaism and history', *Shefa* 2 (1979), pp. 19–37; Greenberg, 'Religious values after the Holocaust: a Jewish view' in Abraham Peck (ed.), *Jews and Christians After the Holocaust* (Philadelphia: Fortress Press, 1982), pp. 63–86.

23. Elie Wiesel, 'Talking and writing and keeping silent' in Franklin Littel and Hubert Locke (eds), *The German Church Struggle and the Holocaust* (Detroit: Wayne State University Press, 1974), pp. 269–77.

24. Eliezer Berkovits, *Faith After the Holocaust* (New York: KTAV, 1973), p. 4. Jonathan Sacks makes a similar point when noting that 'the task of the post-Holocaust generation has been not to speak, but to listen and record': *The Holocaust in Jewish Theology* (Yad Vashem Charitable Trust, 1988), p. 5.
25. Eliezer Berkovits, 'Approaching the Holocaust', *Judaism* 22.1 (1973), pp. 18–20.
26. Berkovits, *Faith After the Holocaust*, p. 69.
27. Berkovits, 'Approaching the Holocaust', p. 19.
28. Eliezer Berkovits, *With God in Hell* (New York: Sanhedrin Press, 1979), p. 96.
29. Emil Fackenheim, *To Mend the World: Foundations of Future Jewish Thought* (New York: Schocken, 1982), p. 9.
30. Shapiro, op. cit., p. 211.
31. Geoffrey Hartman, 'The book of destruction' in Friedlander (ed.), op. cit., pp. 318–34.
32. Elie Wiesel in Philippe de Saint-Cheron and Elie Wiesel, *Evil and Exile* (Notre Dame: University of Notre Dame Press, 1990), p. 9.

7
Where on earth is God?

Rex Ambler

I take it that the question is serious, and that there is no longer an obvious answer. There is no longer much confidence, even among those who believe in God, that we can locate God, either literally or metaphorically. But more than that, it is not any longer clear that there is anywhere, literal or metaphorical, where God could be. All the available space seems to be occupied, taken over largely by human beings and their ever-expanding numbers and activities. By doing for ourselves what we once asked God to do, we have in a sense displaced God. And this could be, as it has been, a matter for some pride and self-confidence. At the same time, though, our godlike activities on earth are presently having a devastating effect on it. We are polluting the elements, eroding the soil, destroying the forests, annihilating species and exhausting the earth's limited resources. Far from having the earth under our providential control, we are damaging it irreparably, without knowing either how to repair the damage or how to stop damaging it to the point of destruction. This is our ecological crisis. And in this crisis, when pride in human achievement can easily turn to disgust and despair, we may well want to cry out, perhaps now with ironic desperation, 'Where on earth is God?'

There is, indeed, some irony in the situation, because the origins of this new kind of godlessness seem to lie within Christianity itself. From the very beginning of our historic faith, humans were given a very special role on the earth, which we could describe as a calling to *represent* God on earth, to exercise at least part of God's rule on earth. Adam and Eve were created 'in God's image', and then called to have dominion over the other creatures of the earth. When humans had clearly failed to fulfil this calling, Jesus, as the 'second

Adam', was called to renew the promise of God's kingdom and to summon men and women to rule with God as his sons and daughters. Eventually, the story then goes, the representative of God took over from God, and God, as Bonhoeffer said, was 'edged out of the world'. We now live 'as if God wasn't there'.[1] But this, suggested Bonhoeffer, was God's purpose all along. God 'allowed himself' to be edged out so that we humans could have the space to grow. He wanted us to outgrow dependency, and in that sense outgrow 'God', so that we could respond to this mystery of our lives as free and mature human beings.

But how, then, is Christian faith, or any faith, still possible? If we cannot trust God in the old way, in a relationship of dependency, is it possible to trust God in any way at all?

Perhaps not. Perhaps faith is no longer possible, except as a faith in ourselves. Perhaps the meaning of our modern history is that we have steadily *internalized* our traditional faith, so that it is we ourselves who have to be trusted because, whether we like it or not, it is we who are in control. This would be the humanist or secularist interpretation, however it is thought through. But that shift in our culture is not simply a loss of faith, as some humanists like to say. For that misses the point that in the end we all have to trust something. It is also a redirection of faith. The rise of the modern outlook, we should say, is essentially a switch of confidence from the great Other to ourselves, so that in the process we could learn to expect from ourselves what we had previously looked to God to provide: whether knowledge, wisdom, purpose, value, support or power. The memory of God above, in his singular power and determination, has remained only as a model for what human beings themselves can become. It is now widely accepted in modern culture that when it comes to the practical problems of life it is we humans who have to analyse the problems and provide the answers. And, until recently, that could seem to many people to be the most rational understanding. There is effectively no God out there telling us what to do or helping us to do it; we are entirely on our own.[2]

This view seems to be confirmed by the situation we are now having to face. The ecological crisis is both world-wide in its scope and literally down-to-earth. It therefore calls for a world-wide understanding and down-to-earth solutions. It does not need religion, either as a sanction for caring or as a guide to action. Indeed, religion could easily be thought to get in the way, because of its other-worldly concerns and its divisive character. It could be argued, then, that if we need any faith to cope with this situation it would have to be a potentially universal secular faith.[3]

But the ecological crisis is now calling even this secular view into question.

It is now all too apparent that our destructive approach to nature comes from an attitude to nature which sees it as essentially different from us, alien to us and potentially hostile as well. This is a distinctly Western attitude, which came to prominence in the seventeenth century to provide the backbone of modern science and modern philosophy.[4] The attitude might have grown out of Christianity in fact, but as internalized in the secular modern it becomes a stark opposition. In order to be able to assume the godlike role of determining knowledge and value for themselves, moderns had to distinguish themselves sharply from the material process of nature, even the nature of their own bodies. They therefore needed something like Descartes' sharp distinction between mind and matter, considered as two wholly different types of substance, to provide a theoretical back-up for their brave new self-confidence. They then had to assert themselves in practice as well as in theory, by bringing nature under their power and by struggling to free their own essential being from its clutches. From then on, the dream of modernity is the dream of freedom, freedom from nature, from tradition, from the past, from everything that is already given and not determined by individual human consciousness. Indeed, everything that is already given has to be destroyed, in order to make room for the new world that we humans will construct.

The ecological crisis is surely telling us that this project is impossible. The long-term effect of our oppositional stance towards nature has been the steady erosion of our own life-support system. It is evident that we cannot fight nature without fighting ourselves: there is no independent ground on which we humans can stand. If we fight nature, we fight it on its own ground and with its own weapons.

Nature is part of us and we are part of it: this seems to be the positive lesson we can draw from the crisis. We live in reciprocal dependency. Nature, therefore, has to be respected in its own right, as a condition of human *self*-respect. We humans have to abandon our attempt to live above the natural order, and learn the humility of being simply part of it. The ultimate goals that humans have set for themselves to guarantee their freedom from nature and the past must be abandoned as illusions, false dreams. The story of our human life can then, perhaps, be rewritten against the backdrop of nature's own story, widening the scope of our action in time and space. Then we shall be able to understand, or begin to understand, the situation we have got ourselves into and the way to get out of it.

I say the ecological crisis is telling us this. In a manner of speaking this is true. But we could say that *God* is telling us this. For what 'speaks' in this critical and dangerous situation is the reality we are ultimately dependent on and which, if we reject it, will finally destroy us and everything we hold dear. I am referring, of course, to the dark reality beyond the crisis, which the crisis will lead us into if we don't consciously turn back. It is not something we can think about very clearly. The annihilation of the human species is the annihilation of all thought and everything that is thinkable. The future of the world without humans is a dark infinity that not even our imaginations can penetrate. And therefore the realization that we are already in the process of bringing about this catastrophic end can, and surely should, fill us with dread. We are encountering the limits of our world and we are peering into a dark abyss. It is a kind of nothingness, that casts a dark shadow on everything we do and hope for, for everything we do is implicated in the process that leads to it. But for that reason this new kind of nothingness is also a kind of reality. The awareness of it can reshape our view of the world. It can provide a test of what we take to be important or real. And since it threatens the reality of everything we take to be real and the value of everything we take to be valuable, it carries an ultimacy that nothing can rival.

I am dwelling on these dark thoughts, you must understand, not in order to depress you, but to highlight the ultimacy of what we are facing here. It seems we cannot understand the critical nature of the present ecological situation without recognizing a new kind of reality which it is opening up before us, namely the ultimate reality of an impenetrable infinity. For the ecological crisis is essentially an experience of limits – the limits of our ecosystem first of all, but also the limits of our human world and the limits of our human freedom. In facing the crisis honestly, we have to look beyond the limits, and what we see is something new and disturbing and incomprehensible. It is, we have to say, the dark side of God.

Could there be another side? If we respond to what is being said in the crisis, redefining ourselves as part of a given, integrated whole, valuing one another and nature as belonging to a creation, we will surely experience a renewal of life and hope. By treating as ultimate in our lives what is in fact ultimate, we shall be liberated from the false ultimates on which much of our modern life has been based, including the ultimate of our own self-consciousness. It is surely, then, possible that what initially struck us as dark and fearsome would come to be seen as a source of light and life. For the darkness of the global threat would have alerted us to a truth about our situation which, if we accept it and live by it, enables us to live more fully.

These reflections on 'the end' therefore, lead us to talk about God after all, even though our talk is somewhat oblique and paradoxical. And they seem to provide an insight on which we could base a theology of the world situation.[5] So much, I hope, we might agree on. We might differ, though, when we come to answer the more specific question with which we started:

where then is God? Where is this voice coming from, this ecological imperative? Where do we place our trust, our priorities, our love? I think there are three possible answers to the question, given that we can no longer think of God as above us, as an all-powerful being: God is beyond, God is here, and God is ahead. I will consider each of these in turn, and then conclude by asking the question how we choose between them.

God is beyond

This is to say that God is not in any imaginable space in the universe, above or below, but wholly beyond it, unimaginable and unthinkable. It is to say that the dark infinity we experience in the ecological crisis *is* God. The experience of God is therefore an experience of the limits of our existence.[6] Subjectively it is an experience of dread, but also, if it is allowed to be, an experience of awe and wonder – for the dark infinity which threatens to engulf us is the infinity out of which we came and which promises to renew our being as creatures of infinity.

To treat this reality as God is to respect the limits around which we experience it, and to accept ourselves as limited within the interconnected world. It is to confess that we are not ultimate, or capable of becoming ultimate, but conditioned by everything with which we are involved; and that what is ultimate is beyond all this conditionedness and connectedness, though it in some way conditions it all.

What we would be hearing, then, in the ecological crisis is a word from beyond the world, telling us to respect the world as a gift and to care for it. In this way it echoes the word of the Bible, which was similarly uttered in times of crisis, when the people's future was at stake. That word, mediated through the prophets and sages, was a call to fear the one origin of their life by respecting the conditions under which their life was possible. 'The fear of the Lord is the beginning of wisdom.' But their relationship with the Origin was not simply given with the conditions of their life. It was established historically, as the people became aware of the possibilities before them and their responsibility for realizing them. They entered into a 'covenant' with their 'Lord', a contractual agreement, in which the Lord promised them life and blessing if they in turn fulfilled his law, but death and devastation if they did not. And the nub of the law was that the people should care for one another, so that all may flourish together, and that they should care for the earth and its creatures, to sustain them in the future. Humans were therefore given not only responsibility for themselves, in that they had to choose between life and death, but also responsibility for the other creatures around them. It was a unique role that they were given to play, and, as we have seen, a role fraught with danger.

Could this prophetic word prove to have a message for us too? If the crisis in our human relationship with the earth can be thought to be establishing an implicit covenant for us, so that once again we humans are faced with a historic choice between life and death, then surely that word is relevant again. We could, then, interpret that word for our time in such a way that it clarifies our unique human responsibility for ourselves and our world. We could also give it a specifically Christian emphasis, by showing how Jesus enacted that implicit covenant in his own life and made the historic promise of life realizable through personal faith and love.[7]

But there are also reasons to doubt that this is the best way forward. The idea of God being proposed here is still the idea of a separate, transcendent reality, wholly other than the world, other than us. And it can be doubted whether faith in such a reality can nourish the kind of love and care for the earth that it obviously needs. The trouble is that putting our faith in something wholly other in order to save ourselves or our earth divides our loyalties. We will come to think of ourselves as belonging to the earth, but also to something beyond it. Alternatively, we will come to think of the transcendent God as the only ultimately important reality, and our spiritual life will then be conceived as an ascent to God, away from the earth.[8] The earth and its creatures will then be conceived as having no value in themselves, only a value as a means to the realization of something else, which, of course, then lays them open to exploitation. Such an ambivalence towards nature, it could be said, is precisely what made the present crisis possible in the first place.

God is here

Doubts about the first model have led some religious thinkers to develop a quite different view. This says that God is not a separate, distant reality, but part of the reality of our everyday life. God is not beyond, but here, in this place, in this moment. But God is not present as an object is present. God is eternal, so God is present to us in another dimension than our familiar dimensions of space and time. The dimension of God cuts through our time and space *in* the present moment – rather as a line can cut through the centre of a two-dimensional circle, if the line is in the third dimension. But how is such a thing knowable? Only as we are able to let go our normal preoccupation with people and events, and relax into a state of openness, which means of course letting go the preoccupations of the self. When we abandon the self-centred viewpoint we are able to see God in the world, and the world in God.

This, as you will recognize, is the classic view of the mystical tradition, of all mystical traditions. But transposed into an ecological key it sounds rather different. It is now not only an affirmation of God (in the world), but also an affirmation of the world (in God). It is not only possible to love God in the world, but also to love the world in God. This shift of emphasis, then, marks it off from the kind of mysticism that seeks an escape from the world. More in the tradition of Francis of Assisi or Hildegard of Bingen, it is a positively earth-loving spirituality.

But more than that, it is an earth-caring spirituality. In thinkers like Matthew Fox and Thomas Berry a mystical awareness is wakened by and shaped by a sense of the earth's need.[9] It therefore has a strongly practical impetus, to save the earth, and ourselves with it. It could be said here, then, that the voice that speaks in the ecological crisis is believed to come from the earth itself. The cry of the earth is the voice of God. But in this case it is not a harsh voice of judgement, threatening devastation. It is a soft voice, pleading, persuading. It seeks to win our love. And the human experience that answers to it is the delight of recognition, or the joy of coming home. For the recognition of God in the world is the discovery that the earth is, after all, our true home; that, for all our ignorance and alienation, we are embraced by God in simply being alive. If there is fear and anxiety as well, or instead, then this should be understood as an experience of alienation or lostness, which will in its own way – like the 'dark night of the soul' – lead us back to the joy of real unity.

There is a strong note of celebration in this earthy spirituality. It is affirming the goodness of life as more fundamental than its evils. It is affirming the unity of life, of all reality, as more fundamental than its fragmentations and oppositions. But, wholesome and sound as that affirmation is, it does raise a question that could lead us to cast doubt on this whole way of thinking. The question is whether it takes the fragmentations and oppositions in life seriously enough. There is a mystical experience of unity, I have no doubt. But we have to recognize that it occurs as the normal experience of a responsible self is suspended. There is always, then, the problem – not insurmountable, I'm sure – of how to relate that vision to the experience of everyday life. One way of resolving this problem is to point out, as Matthew Fox does for example, that we are just as interconnected in our everyday life as we are in the mystic vision. The new ecological conception of the world as a single integrated process, coupled with the new cosmology which construes human life and consciousness as integral to the cosmic process (rather than as a freak exception), tends to confirm the mystic understanding. They may indeed be compatible, but I would hesitate to say they were actually the same thing. To put it simply, a unity of process is not the same as a unity of being. But, more to the point, neither can be equated with our everyday experience of the world, where we are bound to experience ourselves, and other people, as individual responsible agents. And this sense of ourselves as separate and distinct is a practical necessity. It is because of this, we might think, that we have problems in our relationship with nature: we are obviously part of it in one sense, but in another sense we are obviously not. There seems to be an inescapable loneliness in the human situation. At any rate, there is an actual loneliness: over centuries, with the growth of our cities and technologies, we have developed our life in a struggle with nature, foolishly or not, so that we cannot now conceive ourselves as simply part of it. And our problem is not an individual one merely, that is, it is not a problem that can be satisfactorily overcome by a change of individual consciousness. It is also a social and cultural problem. What is required to bring us into harmony with nature has to be a (very big) social and cultural transformation.

God is ahead

The previous two answers to the question, where is God?, leave us with a dilemma: where are *we*? If God is beyond the world, we are stranded between the two. If God is here in the world, one with nature, we are immersed in nature. The ecological crisis is telling us, no doubt, that that, in a sense, is where we belong, but that is not where we are. The crisis is precisely that we are altogether in the wrong place. Our whole human world is at odds with the natural world; and until they are brought into harmony, in practical actuality, there is no long-term hope for either of them. The unity and harmony we are looking for does not therefore exist, and, in a sense, never has done.

In this respect, our third alternative is different from the other two in a quite fundamental way. They both consider that the unity we are looking for already exists, waiting only to be discovered and affirmed by us. In the one case it is a unity of creation, an order or structure given by God. In the second it is a unity of all being, of all life, in which God and the world are united. But in both cases the unity is already established. Only human beings are out of step, and that because of their ignorance or self-preoccupation. If and when they can be made to realize the truth, they will experience this unity for themselves. This, I think, is the expectation. In our third alternative, however, the unity being envisaged cannot be thought of as already existing, because it is a unity between two worlds that have always, until now, been in conflict. If the human and natural worlds are able to come together and resolve the conflict, it will be something quite new. It will no doubt recall that early moment in our history, before we built cities and civilizations, when we seemed to be at one with our environment, rather as the biblical dream of a new kingdom of God echoes the paradise in Eden (Rev 22.1–5). But it will not, and will not be able to, recapitulate it. Our struggle with nature over the millennia has changed everything. We have lost many chances, but also created new ones. And along with the new bleak chance that we could destroy human life if we so chose, there is a new bright chance that we could re-create it so that that danger is removed. The two chances belong together: the positive possibility is simply the obverse of the negative one. Just because we have the power to destroy the world, we have the power to re-create it. But also, if we seriously wish to avoid the negative outcome, we have to work for the positive one. The situation is so critical that we seem no longer to have the option of a compromise between the two. This means that the ecological imperative that we discussed before turns out to be a promise as well as a threat. It says that if we do what has to be done, we will not only escape destruction, but also enter into a new experience of life which will come close to the realization of our deepest dreams.

What is also distinctive about this new unity of the human and the natural, this new community of earthly life, is that it has to be created. It needs the unique human power of creativity to bring it about, but at the same time it needs a sense of identity with the earth for humans to know what kind of a community they have to build. In this respect it calls for *both* a prophetic sense of human responsibility *and* a mystic sense of oneness with all life, but now transformed into an active, creative mode, a praxis of the love and nurture of life.

Where, then, is God in all this? God is not part of any given order or structure, since the existing world can find itself only in the emergence of something new. God is therefore mediated through the new possibilities that can inspire us to bring that about. God is ahead. God comes to us, not so much out of the past, calling us back to where we were, but out of the future, beckoning us to a new world, that we ourselves must help to create.[10] God answers to our freedom and responsibility, our unique way of being, but also to our longing for unity and life, which binds us with all creatures. So God is the creative source of our life, that lures us into becoming what we have it in us to become, but in such a way as to enhance, rather then limit, our freedom and creativity.

It may be thought that this view is too idealistic, too utopian. How can we dare to have that kind of hope, when most of our experience tends to run against it? This is a fair point. To sustain hope we need to have an experience of life that convinces us that the failures of life, and of history, need not have the last word. We need, perhaps, an experience of life which is close to the mystic experience, which transcends the ordinary and the everyday. At the same time, while cherishing grounds for hope, we need to be able to face the possibility of failure, even the possibility of failing to save the planet. Here, perhaps, we need the prophetic insight that our lives do not have to succeed in order to be meaningful; that it is possible to find meaning and fulfilment in commitment to what is hoped for, even if what is hoped for doesn't eventually happen. What would be important is faithfulness to the vision.

If these qualifications are accepted, then it appears that we do not, after all, have to choose between the three possible views. We could draw on all of them, as and when needed, even if it were not possible to harmonize them intellectually. But that incongruity might actually be helpful. It could remind us that God is, first of all, a reality to be trusted, rather than to be understood.

Notes

1. Dietrich Bonhoeffer, *Letters and Papers from Prison* (SCM Press, 1953 and subsequently).
2. John Passmore has articulated this view in relation to the ecological crisis in his *Man's Responsibility for Nature* (2nd edn, Duckworth, 1980).
3. On the significance of this concept, see Annette Baier, 'Secular faith' in Terence Penelhum (ed.), *Faith* (Macmillan, 1989), pp. 226–42.
4. Cf. Carolyn Merchant, *The Death of Nature* (2nd edn, Harper and Row, 1989).
5. At this point I am following a line of thought developed by Jürgen Moltmann in *The Theology of Hope* (SCM Press, 1967), where he suggests that talk of God can be renewed by contemplating the future. I have made an attempt at a 'theology of the world situation' in my *Global Theology* (SCM Press, 1990).
6. Cf. the essay 'Transcendence without mythology' in Gordon Kaufman, *God the Problem* (Harvard University Press, 1972).
7. On the relevance of the biblical theme of covenant to present-day ecological theology, see Robert Murray, *The Cosmic Covenant* (Sheed and Ward, 1992).
8. On the historic appeal of the spirituality of 'ascent' in Christianity, see H. Paul Santmire, *The Travail of Nature* (Philadelphia: Fortress Press, 1985).
9. E.g. Matthew Fox, *Creation Spirituality* (New York: HarperCollins, 1991); and Thomas Berry, *The Dream of the Earth* (Sierra Club Books, 1988).
10. I remember the excitement I felt when I first came across this idea, in Harvey Cox's essay 'Ernst Bloch and the pull of the future' in Martin E. Marty (ed.), *New Theology*, no. 5 (Collier Macmillan, 1968). Cox was referring of course to Ernst Bloch's massive *Principle of Hope*, now translated into English (Blackwell, 1990). Jürgen Moltmann developed Bloch's ideas theologically in, e.g., *The Theology of Hope* (SCM Press, 1967) and *Hope and Planning* (SCM Press, 1971), but not in relation to the ecological crisis. Nor has anyone else, so far as I know. John B. Cobb comes close to it in, e.g., Cobb and Herman E. Daly, *For the Common Good* (Greenprint, 1990), as does Rosemary Ruether in *God and Gaia* (SCM Press, 1993).

8

'Not through the sound of thunder'. The quest for God in the backyard of history

Werner Ustorf

'Dare we speak of God in public' – is that an invitation or a question? And why should it be daring? Is there something that could prevent this group, included in the corporate 'we', from frankly addressing God in public? Reasons given so far are, on the one hand, the privatization of religion in modern society; on the other, however, the nationalization, or even, tribalization, of religion in terms of 'the Christian heritage of Britain'. There are obviously people in the Department of Education who 'dare' to speak, though it may be doubtful whom they speak of. Perhaps it is the theologians, then, the professional God-talkers, who have problems in speaking of God in public. There is a considerable difficulty, indeed: do we speak of ourselves, or of God? Theologians, particularly, are afraid that all our attempts to listen to God might end up in listening to ourselves only. There is at least a terrible ambiguity. Some say that it is possible to discover only retrospectively the footprints of God, as it were, crossing our way; but that it is impossible to pin-point God as such. Some prefer to postpone the problem altogether. They say, we do not know; but one day, in the eschatological future, we will know.

I have tried to listen to my 'self', and for the purpose of this chapter to *liberate* that part of my self which usually is under theological control. Now this part – let us call him, for the sake of convenience, 'Theodore' (I always wanted to be somebody else) – clearly says *I don't like* to be told that the desire to see the face of God is hopeless. Theodore represents a person – *persona*, or *prosopon* in Greek, meaning 'mask' – which is under the mask and which is made an underdog by another person of my self. However, Theodore is as real as this other person, and he (or me) wants to *see* and to be in direct communion with God. Theodore is not satisfied with the sophisticated knowledge of the other person, telling him to be happy with questionable images, delicate analogy, with shaky metaphors and preliminary symbols only, in brief with the hopeless limitation of the human condition. *This* person of my self shall be equally entitled to participate in the God-talk.

I have a suspicion, and, if it is right, there will be an additional reason to unmask what has been made an underdog. My suspicion is that there is a sort of correspondence between the internal and the external, between the life inside and outside of our skin. What I mean is that the suppression of the internal 'Theodore' could seduce me into agreeing to the suppression of the millions of external Theodores of history. It is not a rhetorical question to ask whether the Western project of dominance and oppression since 1492 was related to the domestication of the Western soul, and the colonization of the quest for God within. Is it possible that one's ability to listen to the voice within, or to see God, is diminished, or even blocked, the more one's self is at home in the certainties of a given culture and religion? Uncertainty and ignorance, then, would be a precondition for an attentiveness that goes beyond the answers culture and religion normally provide. In other words, there is, perhaps, a significant relationship between the liberation of the internal and the external, of 'Theodore' and the quest of those on the underside of history to have God in no uncertain terms on their side. I do not want to make a theory out of this and present a cheap formula for how to change the world. Liberation is a gift. 'Seeing God' means liberation, in my view, and 'Liberator' was precisely the name Ignatius of Loyola attributed to God after he had his vision. We shall return to Ignatius below.

Acknowledging one's own ignorance can at least help to understand others better. The attempts of Western theologians and those from the so-called Third World to communicate, in the sense of understanding each other, ended in the early 1970s in what was called 'incommunication', a euphemism for catastrophe. Third World theologians thought it necessary to establish their own forum for discussion, therefore excluding Westerners. The first assembly of the Ecumenical Association of Third World Theologians issued the following statement in 1976:

> We reject as irrelevant an academic type of theology, that is diverted from action. We are prepared for a radical break in epistemology which makes commitment the first act of theology and engages in critical reflection on the praxis of reality of the Third World . . . Theology for centuries did not seriously contest the plunder of continents, and even the extermination

> of whole peoples and civilizations. The meaning of the message of Jesus Christ was so blunted as not to be sensitive to the agony of whole races.[1]

Did a particular Western Christian image of God, and a particular Western way of doing theology, correspond, as some say, to 'a totalitarian ambition to control the whole of reality', or, as others say, to a 'patriarchal colonial project'?[2] Whose theology are we dealing with? Christianity is a universal faith, not the possession of certain North Atlantic tribes. So, who owns theology? If theology does not arise out of the experiences of the people, whether in this or in other parts of the world, if a substantial amount of current Christian experience is regarded as beyond the pale, it becomes, indeed, either oppressive or unimportant.[3] What John Pobee says about African independent churches seems to be true for a good deal of Christian experience in the West as well:

> Their (hi)story is often told in the form of a story, mostly unwritten. But it is often the story of manifestations of the power of God in healing, exorcism and glossolalia, precisely gifts which Christ bequeathed to His church, but which somehow is put in abeyance by established Christianity. It may not be erudite . . . but it is the history of a church living in time and space, living the biblical faith and addressing the hopes and fears of people.[4]

People usually try to resist the forces of dehumanization; they long for peace, justice and joy. And they are, in a certain way, suspicious of the institutionalized religion, the elaborate faith-system, that uses speculative and abstract philosophy in order to develop its universalistic claim. 'Popular' or 'folk' religion is usually distinguished from 'official' or 'elitist' religion along institutional, socio-cultural and intellectual lines. If one takes official religion to be 'those prescribed beliefs and norms of an institution promulgated and monitored by a group of religious specialists, then popular religion becomes those patterns of behaviour and belief that somehow escape the control of the institutional specialists'.[5] Often it is understood or misunderstood in terms of a belief system, whereas it is more a way of life. Popular religion disturbs the intellectuals' need for a harmonized or controllable world-view. It is very likely therefore that popular religion does not fit into the categories which the dominant or intellectual class has prepared for it. The religions of so-called ordinary people consist usually of simple expectations in relation to life: that one has to eat, that the crop is good or employment continues, that the child regains health, that debt will not become intolerable and war does not threaten, that one has people to talk to, that one stays alive and will die peacefully, having a decent burial. The people's religious discourse is often very careful not to go beyond one's own authority: they do not try to 'explain' or to 'know' or even to define God. But often they would insist that the promises of the tradition, e.g. of the Bible, are verbatim, literally true: they suffer too much, and cannot allow themselves to sacrifice the literal sense of the promise. For the theologians, the human being, in principle, is tragically estranged from God: for impoverished people, all their life is a chain of tragedy and estrangement. 'God' is often the only place they have, and it is an unsafe place. One of the many contributions of Third World theology is the rediscovery of the importance of the richness of people's experience – and I apply the term 'people' in the widest sense. The life of the people is the important thing, and the usefulness of theology, then, depends strongly on how far she can contribute to life. The character of theology therefore is functional.[6]

What I will attempt in this chapter (and, as it should be for someone coming from Heidelberg, it is free of jokes) is to plead for paying more attention to religious experience in our attempts to do theology, in order to help in making us and theology more human. I shall focus on some cases where people claim to have seen God. These cases may not be representative, but they will illustrate the issue. Such experiences within modern culture, and also within academic theology, have a 'marginal' status only. They are usually neglected, and sometimes silenced. They are in the 'backyard' of contemporary Western culture and of history. That is what they have in common with the struggles for survival and for a decent life of people marginalized here and in the non-Western world. I am taking my examples from all these fields.

The African theologian St Augustine and his mother Monica, tired and exhausted from a journey, were standing leaning out of a window overlooking a garden, at Ostia on the Tiber, perhaps in the year 388 CE. Physical and psychic exhaustion in connection with an epiphany of 'nature' have a prominent place in religious experience, as we will see. Augustine was 33, and had a very intimate relationship with his mother who was 56 and, because of an illness, already bearing the mark of death. They talked about the life beyond and eternity – things the human mind in principle could not grasp, as they were quite aware. However, in the desire for union with God they attempted, to the limit of their mental capacity, to think eternity, and something very surprising indeed was happening: it worked!

> Step by step we climbed beyond all corporeal objects and the heaven itself . . . We moved up beyond them so as to attain to the region of inexhaustible abundance.

I am not going into the question of whether it is a recommendable procedure to do it together with Mum; however, Augustine assures us of the fact that both of them, for a flash of a moment, touched truth itself, eternal wisdom itself! In other words: God! How were they able to get that far? The 'method' was 'a moment of total concentration of the heart'. Augustine actually tries to 'explain' the process: it is (my words) the technique of 'switching off' all the noises, whether they are made by the senses, the mind, the soul, or even by the heavens; and when there is no sound, no language, no imagination and no sign, then there is only the sound of God:

> We would hear his word, not through the tongue of flesh, nor through the voice of an angel, nor through the sound of thunder, nor through the obscurity of a symbolic utterance. Him who in these things we love we would hear in person without their mediation.[7]

Another theologian, more than 1,600 years later, did not like that. Karl Barth accuses Augustine of pretending to have seen God face to face, i.e. without an image, without a word or a sign, and without the help of any concept of thought. Why is this an accusation? It is because, as Barth thinks, we cannot get away from symbolic thinking. Where, for that matter, do we leave our gender during worship? It is there, even during prayer, and also in our visions. In fact, Augustine had been criticized for using erotic language in his theology. As human beings, we are hopeless, we never reach God. God only offers God to be heard and seen in revelation. We must not seek where God is not to be found; God seeks us in the words of the Bible, as Barth says.[8]

Karl Barth holds that all religion, Christian religion included, basically is unbelief.[9] Religion as such, with all its images and symbols, is a human construction, the shell of self-protection, and therefore in principle hostile to God. The distance existing between God and humanity is unmeasurable, and religious language does not decrease this gulf, but in fact increases it in terms of the increase of an illusion. There is no way for humans to see God – Augustine has got it all wrong. The Danish philosopher Søren Kierkegaard categorically tells us that 'it is blasphemous to fraternize with God'.[10] As we have heard, the argument continues by giving God the full initiative – God makes God known or seen. The technical term for this is 'revelation'.

Who defines what is revelation and what is not? As far as it is part of 'religion', revelation too is the product of human self-deception, and Barth's example is Augustine's vision in Ostia. On the other hand, if 'revelation' really is beyond religion, if it is the sound of God, then we have in fact come full circle. We arrive again at the point of departure, namely the historical fact that people throughout history have claimed that they have seen or heard nothing less than God, i.e. revelation – the case in point again is Augustine. Barth's distinction between religion and revelation is helpful, but it is tautological at the same time: it does not solve the problem, but it is an indication of the problem. What is the nature of this problem?

Genesis 32 reports Jacob's wrestling with an enigmatic being at the Jabbok river. Jacob is not really overcome, but certainly seriously weakened – the sinew of his thigh is dislocated by this 'someone'. During the fight, however, Jacob will not let his opponent go, but surprisingly wants his blessing, and indeed forces this stranger to bless him. Who was this strange 'someone'? The book of Genesis gives its own answer by letting us know that Jacob later called the place of the wrestling 'Pniel' (face of God): 'For I have seen God face to face and I am still living.' Jacob's new name, Israel, explicitly refers to this story: 'Thou hast striven with God and with men and hast prevailed.'

This story certainly shows the problem in its peculiar twilight. One can ask whether our relation to transcendence really is a love story, as some may think, or whether it is more like a dangerous duel. Where one stands utterly against God and nevertheless asks for his blessing, there, as Barth would say, the epiphany of God may occur. Another question is the narration's fascinating display of human and divine interaction to the degree of symbiosis. There is no other text in the Hebrew Bible where a human being can force God to give a blessing. That it is man who is the more active part reminds us again of the vision of Augustine. But what is of most interest *here* is the ambiguity of this strange 'someone'.[11] In the encounter itself Jacob does not really *know* whom he has to face. Is it a member of a different ethnic group, claiming territorial prerogatives? Is this 'someone' the syncretistic echo of the merger of the God of Abraham with a pre-existing local God or demon? Perhaps a night demon of the Jabbok river: he could not stand daylight, and had to try to escape before sunrise?[12] At dawn a human could blackmail the demon: 'Bless me, or you are going to be killed.' Obviously, it was *this* interpretation the prophet Hosea (12.4–5) referred to. Hosea's conclusion is that one cannot deal with *God* how Jacob did – when he met the *angel*. The wrestling at Jabbok, then, shows how Israel must not deal with God. Hosea, then, is criticizing Jacob in a similar way to that in which Barth criticized Augustine. But how can Hosea, as well as Barth, know that Jacob, or Augustine, in fact had not seen God? How can we know whether it is a 'someone', a demon, a stranger, an angel, an illusion, a projection, wishful thinking, the image of our own madness, or God who is approaching us?

* * *

I will illustrate the question by referring to a cultural background as far as possible from our own: Japan. In 1938 the Japanese ecologist Masanobu Fukuoka had a spontaneous intuitive insight into reality while he was at Yokohama. It came after a serious and drawn-out bout of pneumonia, and a period of depression which continued after his release from hospital. He writes:

> One night as I wandered, I collapsed in exhaustion on a hill overlooking the harbour, finally dozing against the trunk of a large tree. I lay there, neither asleep nor awake, until dawn. I can still remember that it was the morning of the 15th of May. In a daze I watched the harbour grow light, seeing the sunrise and yet somehow not seeing it. As the breeze blew up from the bluff, the morning mist suddenly disappeared. Just at that moment a night heron appeared, gave a sharp cry, and flew away into the distance. I could hear the flapping of its wings. In an instant all my doubts and the gloomy mist of my confusion vanished. Everything I held in firm conviction, everything upon which I had ordinarily relied was swept away with the wind. I felt that I understood just one thing. Without my thinking about them, words came from my mouth: 'In this world there is nothing at all. . . .' I felt that I understood nothing.

To 'understand nothing' in the Japanese context is not only to recognize the insufficiency of intellectual knowledge; it is the claim to have come to understand *nothingness* itself, and, as a result, to be able to identify nothingness. Fukuoka continues.

> I could see that all the concepts to which I had been clinging, the very notion of existence itself, were empty fabrications. My spirit became light and clear. I was dancing wildly for joy. I could hear the small birds chirping in the trees, and see the distant waves glistening in the rising sun. The leaves danced green and sparkling. I felt that this was truly heaven on earth. Everything that had possessed me, all the agonies, disappeared like dreams and illusions, and something one might call 'true nature' stood revealed.[13]

Decades later, Fukuoka identified this experience as an encounter with God: 'One day while still a young man', he says, 'I saw suddenly the totality of God.'[14] In Buddhist tradition, the terms 'totality of God' and 'nothingness' are both equal in value to the term 'true reality', and in one publication Fukuoka explicitly referred to the experience as having achieved enlightenment in the same sense that the Buddha did: he was certain 'that the wisdom that I had attained was not even slightly different from the wisdom known by Shakyamuni'. Interestingly enough, many Buddhists would take a

'Barthian' stand, as it were, and would take the very claim to have achieved enlightenment as good evidence that one has not.[15] In any case, what matters for the moment is that the experience of transcendence calls for interpretation. And it seems that the interpretation is made from those elements of tradition that are culturally and religiously at hand, and that do correspond to the respective experience. Ignatius of Loyola will be the case helping us to understand the mechanics of the process of interpretation.

In the *Report of the Pilgrim*, his autobiography of 1555, Ignatius gives an account of an experience which he himself considered to be decisive and which changed his life. During 1522, Ignatius lived through a period of spiritual crisis and depression which forced him to spend more than a year in Manresa, a small town not far from Barcelona. Outside Manresa, above the valley of the river Cardoner, Ignatius had his mystical experience. He refers to himself in the third person:

> Absorbed in devotion he walked along, then sat down for a while at a place overlooking the river flowing on deep down. Being seated the eyes of his mind did open. Not that he had seen a particular apparition, but he received as a gift the perception and the knowledge of many things in terms of spiritual life and as well of the truths of faith and human understanding. This was accompanied by such a great enlightenment that everything appeared to him in a new light . . . This event was so affirmative that his mind remained as if illuminated. And he thought he had become a different man.[16]

Ignatius ever after was 'a man seized and possessed by God' as Hugo Rahner says.[17] The vision by the Cardoner provided him with the essential elements to be unfolded later in his *Spiritual Exercises*.[18] There can be no doubt that Ignatius had experienced what Rahner calls a 'direct knowledge' of God, a direct knowledge which Ignatius, a converted Christian, then tried to integrate into the theological traditions of the Church. Ignatius was certain of having seen God, i.e. without mediation. Still in 1544 and 1545 he confessed that sometimes his understanding rose up 'without any willing of my own', and in these moments he thought he could 'behold something of the divine Being'. He felt his soul entering the Creator and Lord, once it had managed to get out of the self. This is the background to some of the more audacious words of Ignatius like 'I penetrated in spirit all the mysteries of the Christian faith', or 'Always and at every hour he could find God when he wished'.[19]

However, precisely the non-mediated character of the experience became a problem for Ignatius, and he felt the necessity of transforming the immediacy of his mystical vision into theological contemplation. He in fact suffered from having revelations from 'above', and at the same time from feeling that he had 'no right to look upwards'. Can a human being see God and live? Is there a temptation to take over the place of God? This is the reason why Ignatius emphasized that it is necessary to see one's vision of God *in facie Ecclesiae*, in the light of the teachings of the Church. Decisive for him became Christology, because Christ becomes the mediator, the theological 'missing link', connecting the absoluteness of the 'above' and the limitedness of the 'below'. In other words, the theological 'explanation' of the contradiction is that it is not human powerfulness which reveals God, but God's grace from above, i.e. God's self-revelation in Christ. The incarnation of God in Christ includes the grace of the possibility of the mystical vision. And now the mystic heights of immediate experience are united with the Church's dogmas. When people are being lifted up to see the face of God the Father, it is because God the Son graciously intercedes. In Ignatius' view, Christ not only becomes the access, the door, to the Father, he also screens off 'the naked light of the Father' (H. Rahner). Humanity, in other words, can directly experience God – and survive this encounter. However, as a Christian one can only do it in and through Christ. This is the interpretation of Ignatius.

Jacob, Ignatius and Fukuoka were landholders, wealthy people; Augustine perhaps was not rich, but he certainly was not a pauper either. Does deprivation prevent us from the great mystical experience, or does it change the content of this experience? In other words, do not only cultural and religious traditions play a role in shaping the interpretational framework of the experience, but also class and the fragmentation of life in an industrialized or a post-industrial society? In a report of 1861 on one of London's slums one can find the following observation:

> 19 Dudley Street, Top Front. An Irish family, extremely poor, no Scriptures, attend occasionally at St Patrick's Chapel. Their children, five in number, are not going to school at all for they are all but naked, two of them are running about with nothing on but rags in the shape of a shirt. 'I wish we were all dead,' said the mother, 'I don't care, we couldn't be worse off than we are now. I don't believe there is a God at all. If there is he don't care much for us I know. May be we have not tried him, but I don't think it will be any use. I wish he would send us a loaf of bread right now.'[20]

This God, or this non-God, as it appears from this woman's statement, obviously is a completely different being from the one experienced by Jacob,

Augustine, Ignatius or Fukuoka. The backyard of history goes beyond the marginalized territories of religious experience. The history of Western culture itself has produced its own backyards here and abroad. The non-experience of God is perhaps the most important religious experience currently in Western culture. That God is hidden, and that it is beyond the human condition to encounter absoluteness: that is a common assumption. We can call it the experience of spiritual loneliness. It means the critical and justified condemnation of one's motivations, one's attitudes and one's faithfulness; in brief, the condemnation of one's very self – theologically speaking, the non-experience of grace and mercy. If there is no experience of grace, how can there be mercy with one's self and with others? But the issue is even wider: Tennyson's line about there being more faith in honest doubt than in half the world's creeds delineates it. Honest doubt has become a 'holy' place in Western culture, and it is not far from the Decalogue's prohibition of engaging in the fabrication of images. The problem is that honest doubt has a very precarious place inside the Church.

It seems to me that the image of the non-image of God, or the experience of the non-experience, or of the silence of God, is one of the loudest noises in Western culture. It will not be sufficient here to 'speak' of God, but to show a way of life where God's presence can be felt.

How can what I would call the God of mercy be experienced in a culture where it is difficult to find mercy? I will give a further example from the immediate present, taken from Brazil:

> In a Recife slum, a woman said to a nun: 'Sister, today God has been to my house!' The nun asked how this was, and was told: 'I had no money to buy medicine for my little boy who is ill. Then, my neighbour was paid for a whole week's washing – 100 cruzeiros. She gave it all to me so that I could buy the medicine. If that's not God, what is?'[21]

What is the relation of the God of mercy, experienced as being present in life, intervening and healing, to the God of the mystical experience? Clearly, we are dealing here with experiences that are different in character. The first is social by nature, arising out of the context of social life and leading back to a renewed form of living in community. The second experience starts off as a highly individualistic event, though it usually triggers off a transformation of the social world as well. It seems to me that the God of mercy has a lot to do with people's religion. There is an awareness of not trying to 'explain' God, but of celebrating God's presence, and living in accordance with God's commandments. A case from twentieth-century Africa may illustrate this.

In 1921 Simon Kimbangu caused a religious mass movement in the then Belgian Congo. He became the prophet and founder figure of the biggest independent church in black Africa – in fact, of a new Christian denomination. Theologically, they are exploring at the moment the question of whether their salvational experience, the teachings and the acts of healing of the prophet Kimbangu, can be understood in terms of a second incarnation; namely the incarnation of the third person of the Trinity, the Holy Spirit, in Kimbangu. Simon Kimbangu was a poor man, and in certain respects an outsider, and he suffered from the destruction colonialism had caused among his people. The common mood was frequently expressed as 'God has forgotten us'. Kimbangu had religious experiences, urging him to heal and to preach. But the missionaries of the time regarded him as stupid and uneducated, and rejected his application to become a catechist; in other words, the missionaries refused to provide an African mystical experience of the merciful God with a legitimate place within the mission church. That is the basic reason for the birth of the independent Kimbanguist Church. Today we have perhaps more than 10,000 independent Christian churches in Africa.

Kimbangu's decisive experience, an audition, the equivalent to a vision with the difference that not seeing but hearing is involved, fortunately had been written down by his secretaries in 1921. It is explicitly linked to the rejection by the missionaries:

> Devastated, he fell into his house, threw himself on the floor and prayed. In a dream he believed he became aware of God's voice. 'I have heard your request. People think that one needs intelligence to do my work, but I will give you something which surpasses this.' There then followed the command to preach and heal as God's Apostle, independently of the agreement of 'these people'.[22]

The merciful God made the country go wild for the next couple of decades. Then, in 1957, a proper 'church' was established, followed in 1977 by a theological seminary, and today we have Kimbanguist theologians who define how the prophet understood himself in 1921.

The experiences we have discussed so far can all be classified as 'direct knowledge', and in most of the cases these experiences have been submitted to interpretation. But it is the power of this direct experience, be it of the God of the mystical union or the God of mercy, which triggers off important historical developments: the importance of Jacob for Judaism is beyond question, though we may wish to exclude his story here for historical reasons; Augustine provided the occidental Church with a theological framework which lasted for nearly a millennium; Ignatius developed new models of how to follow Jesus Christ, and he became one of the founders of the missionary order of the Jesuits; Fukuoka, a learned plant pathologist, contributed greatly to ecological thought, and his books are prominent with those who try to rethink the relation between modern market culture and nature; in Africa, Kimbangu is increasingly understood as an icon of the unmixed and undivided character of the human–divine encounter; and emancipation movements of all kinds, and liberation theology, I think, try to continue in their respective ways the experience or the non-experience of the God of mercy.

How, then, to understand the fact that the public, and also the theological, opinion on the question of a direct knowledge of God is fully divided? That there are men like Augustine, Ignatius and Fukuoka, claiming to having seen God 'face to face', and other circles, like Karl Barth and modern humanist thought, explicitly ruling out such a possibility? And, finally, how to face the biblical evidence which is equally divided on this issue? The man Moses represents both the non-possibility of seeing God face to face, and according to Exodus 24, the bliss of seeing God on Mount Sinai for not less than 40 days – perhaps, apart from the narrative of Adam and Eve, the most prominent case of 'direct knowledge' reported in the Old Testament. The New Testament is broadly in line with this. Paul, the theologian, clearly distinguishes between an indirect and a direct knowledge of God. On the one hand, he claims to have *seen* Jesus (1 Cor 9.1). On the other hand, according to the first two chapters of the letter to the Romans, *creation* itself, and then *human conscience*, are the sources of an indirect, and possibly also salvific form of knowledge of God. Barth, again, does not like that.[23]

These are big questions, and I will only speak for myself in this matter, or for 'Theodore'. How do I see the controversy? The salient point for me is that the Bible itself is ambiguous here, and often confirms that there is a direct knowledge of God; in other words, knowledge that is not mediated. The theological alternative basically is either to declare 'revelation' a monopoly of the Christians, that means to radically reject any other form of direct or indirect knowledge of God, or, alternatively, declare all revelation, all knowledge of God, to be effected and enabled by Christ. The first and exclusivist option usually became powerful during the long period of Christendom. The second option, the inclusivist position, is more related to a multi-faith context. That is the option Paul went for when he defined Jesus the Christ as the window to the Father (Eph 2.18), just as John 14.6 states: 'No one comes to the Father except through me.' That means, in my opinion, that in so far as anyone approaches God – be it Augustine, Ignatius, Fukuoka or even myself – that approach is made possible by Christ It does *not* define, however, the language, religious or cultural, of the approach.[24] It does not say that the Church or Christianity is the exclusive channel of God's salvific activity in the world. And it does not say that the blueprint of the new world, which is to bring creation to its fulfilment, is capitalist democracy. But it invites us to join those who are trying to build up this world, and who are engaged in a long-term project of life, freedom, equality and participation. In other words, what the dispute on the possibility of seeing God face to face is about is not blasphemy versus orthodoxy, but control versus liberation of the religious competence of the people. All theology, and all the Church's dogmas, originally have come from people's experiences. And why should that not remain so?[25]

Conclusion

Epiphanies of the transcendent and the sacred can be misunderstood. They need mediation, they need to be seen in the light of religious tradition and of critical reflection to expound their meaning safely. In Pentecostalism, translators have the job of making sense of the utterings spoken in tongues. But here, precisely, people have to be careful that new experiences are not simply channelled into the safe haven of tradition, and that the process of communication does not follow the rules of the notorious dialogue between Humpty Dumpty and Alice:

> 'There's glory for you!'
> 'I don't know what you mean by "glory",' Alice said.
> Humpty Dumpty smiled contemptuously. 'Of course you don't – till I tell you. I meant "there's a nice knock-down argument for you!"'
> 'But "glory" doesn't mean "a nice knock-down argument",' Alice objected.
> 'When *I* use a word,' Humpty Dumpty said, in rather a scornful tone, 'it means just what I choose it to mean – neither more nor less.'
> 'The question is,' said Alice, 'whether you can make words mean so many different things.'
> 'The question is,' said Humpty Dumpty, 'which is to be master – that's all.'[26]

Christian theology is a discipline which tries coherently and critically to relate and explore the Christian tradition, the history of the Church, and the ongoing experience of the faith. Currently, and I have to say that self-critically, theology still has difficulties in regarding people's experiences as an important starting-point for doing theology. The danger is that, by neglecting what people across history have experienced or not experienced, 'we', the theologians, cease to speak of God, or that we behave just like the missionaries did in the Congo in 1921. Then theology could become a sort of Humpty Dumpty, and the people might look somewhere else for the bread of life; and then it is the theologians who may be in the backyard of history.

Notes

1. Cf. the documentation ed. by S. Torres and V. Fabella, *The Emergent Gospel: Theology from the Developing World* (London: Geoffrey Chapman, 1978)
2. L. Morren, quoted in *Theology in Context* (1990–91), p. 142; G. Dietrich, *Bangalore Theological Forum* 21 (1989), pp. 1–29.
3. John Roxborogh, 'Whose history and whose theology?', *Mission Studies* 15 (1991), pp. 93–103.
4. John Pobee, 'Oral theology and Christian oral tradition', *Mission Studies* 11 (1989), pp. 88–9.
5. Cf. R. J. Schreiter, *Constructing Local Theologies* (London: SCM Press, 1985), pp. 122–43; Arnaldo Nesti, 'Gramsci et la religion populaire', *Social Compass* 22 (1975), pp. 343–54.
6. Cf. *East Asian Pastoral Review* 26/1 (1989), pp. 51–72.
7. Augustine, *Confessions,* trans. Henry Chadwick (Oxford: OUP, 1992), IX, x (23–25), or pp. 170–2. Cf. also Paul Henry, *The Path to Transcendence* (Pittsburgh, 1981).
8. Karl Barth, *Church Dogmatics*, ed. G. W. Bromiley and T. F. Torrance (Edinburgh: T. & T. Clark, 1965), II.1, pp. 10–11.
9. Ibid., I.2, section 17, p. 299.
10. *Einübung im Christentum*, by 'Anti-Climacus' ed. S. Kierkegaard (Copenhagen, 1850).
11. Cf. Walter Hollenweger, *Interkulturelle Theologie* (Munich: Kaiser), II (1982), pp. 112–2, and III (1988), pp. 226–32. His interpretation of Genesis 32 is based on Claus Westermann's commentary on Genesis (3 vols, Neukirchen, 1974–82).
12. Cf. Walter Beyerlin (ed.), *Religionsgeschichtliches Textbuch zum Alten Testament* (2nd edn, Göttingen: Vandenhoeck & Ruprecht, 1985), I, p. 266.
13. M. Fukuoka, *The One Straw Revolution* (Emmaus, PA: Rodale Press, 1978), pp. 8–9, quoted by Michael Seigel, 'Mission and ecology: an exercise in dialogue and contextualisation' (PhD thesis, University of Birmingham, 1992), pp. 61–4.
14. M. Fukuoka, *The Road Back to Nature* (Tokyo: Japan Publications, 1987), p. 17, quoted by M. Seigel, op. cit., p. 63.
15. M. Fukuoka, *Mu no Tetsugaku* (Tokyo: Shunjusha, 1985), pp. 267–8, quoted, translated and commented on by M. Seigel, op. cit., pp. 64–5.
16. Cf. Friedhelm Mennekes and Joseph Beuys, *Manresa. Eine Aktion als geistliche Übung zu Ignatius von Loyola* (Frankfurt/M. and Leipzig: Insel, 1992), p. 31. My own translation.
17. Hugo Rahner, *Ignatius the Theologian* (London: Geoffrey Chapman, 1968; paperback edn 1990), p. 2.
18. Ignatius of Loyola, *Spiritual Exercises* (Paulist Press, 1991).
19. Quoted by Rahner, op. cit., pp. 4ff.
20. Quoted by Hugh McLeod, 'The dechristianisation of the working class in Western Europe (1850–1900)', *Social Compass* 27.2/3 (1980), pp. 191–214 (p. 211).
21. Quoted by Kosuke Koyama, 'New world – new creation', *Mission Studies*, X/1&2 (1993), pp. 59–77 (p. 61).
22. Quoted by W. Ustorf, *Christianized Africa – De-Christianized Europe? Missionary*

Inquiries into the Polycentric Epoch of Christian History (Seoul: Tyrannus Press, 1993), p. 50; based on Paul Raymaekers (ed.), *L'Histoire de l'Apparition du Prophète Simon Kimbangu d'après les écrivains Nfinangani et Nzungu* (Kinshasa, 1971).
23. Karl Barth, op. cit., II/1, p. 119.
24. In this question, I go along with Peter Cotterell, 'The unevangelized: an olive branch from the opposition', *International Review of Mission* 82 (1998), pp. 131–5.
25. I am aware of the fact that the position I have taken implies much wider questions than I have addressed in this chapter. One could summarize my position in the following way, and at the same time describe the fields waiting for further exploration:
(a) 'revelation' (as discussed above) is a continuing, or, a permanently ongoing process; (b) revelation occurs with people, all people, ordinary people included – therefore, it cannot be defined by theologians only; (c) revelation produces a plurality of expressions of truth; (d) revelation is not just information about the cosmos and about how to lead one's life (revelation is in a different class from reason, science or philosophy, and ethics); revelation responds to the dimension of meaning, of depth and ultimate concern in being human.
26. Lewis Carroll, *Through the Looking Glass* (1896), ch. VI. I owe this to the recently published book by William Hamilton, *A Quest for the Post-Historical Jesus* (London: SCM Press, 1993), p. 8.

9

'What is truth?' Rehabilitating Pontius Pilate

Gareth Jones

In 1841, on succeeding to Hegel's chair of philosophy in Berlin, Schelling announced his first lecture with unmistakable intent: 'Gentlemen, I am aware of the importance of this moment.'[1] Thus began the last attempt in modern thought to establish a philosophy of revelation grounded in the conviction that truth is a historical quality, a matter of immanence; i.e. something to be encountered *positively*, in the world, rather than as a transcendental condition or category of thought. Though Christian theology since Schweitzer has constantly returned to this question, interpreting eschatological motifs by analogy with differing models of human existence – consider, for example, Bultmann and Heidegger in the 1920s, or Moltmann and Ernst Bloch in the 1960s – only Pannenberg since Schelling has attempted to understand revelation in terms of historical *process*; and even Pannenberg did not reduce the question of truth itself to an item of temporal index.[2] For better or for worse, and despite the priority of immanentist critique in modern theology, the question of truth, Pilate's question (John 18.38), has remained a question of *transcendence* for Christian faith seeking understanding. This is the world in which we live and work, those of us who ask questions of truth and method as systematically as possible, and thereby as doctrinal interpretation.

It follows from this introduction that I am not concerned with a *philosophical* discussion of theories of truth, of consensus, coherence, and correspondence. On the contrary, as a systematic theologian I am operating with a *confessional* theory of truth, one which understands truth as itself established in witness and testimony, and therefore as something contextual.[3] This has profound implications for the way in which one understands the truth of

Christianity *vis-à-vis* other religions, and thereby profound implications for the way in which one speaks of God in public *within* a context of religious pluralism, such as contemporary European society. What I want to do in this chapter is to argue for the doctrinal basis of such a confessional understanding of truth, against the background of modernity – hence my beginning with Schelling.

Notwithstanding his significance in the story of German philosophy, however, Schelling's thought is a purposive genesis for a discussion of Christian truth claims in modernity for a very different reason. As stated, Schelling was reacting explicitly against Hegel; reacting, therefore, not solely against the claims of and for absolute reason in society, but also against the priority of Hegel's understanding of power and human agency.[4] More specifically, Schelling attacked the notion that, consequent to a dynamic of mental evolution, power as transcendent or pure concept was somehow available to human, social appropriation. On the contrary, Schelling argued, one recognizes the irruption of power into the world *through* the world – for example, in nature, in history, in the great events of time, in religious experience – a contrast with Hegel's philosophy which highlights a point of vital importance and distinction for modern thought: does one, with Hegel, argue for the harnessing of the world, of transcendence and immanence, through the exercise of rational power; or does one, with Schelling, argue for the world's power over *humanity*, for the priority of time and experience, of *revelation* in time and experience, over any attempt to exploit it? Hegel's path has led, directly and indirectly, to capitalism, dialectical materialism, modern sociology, and the ideology of Western consumerism – a point made most recently by Francis Fukuyama's *The End of History and the Last Man*.[5] Schelling's path, by contrast, encounters Kierkegaard, Nietzsche and Heidegger along the way – figures who prioritize not human power and agency, but rather the contingency of all historical existence.

Modern reflection apart from philosophy has recognized the validity of the Schellingian argument: one thinks, for example, of texts such as Robert Musil's *The Man Without Qualities*, Marcel Proust's *Remembrance of Things Past*, Thomas Mann's *The Magic Mountain*, Hermann Hesse's *The Glass Bead Game*, T. S. Eliot's *The Waste Land*, and Elias Canetti's masterpiece *Auto da Fe*, each of which emphasizes the transfigured and fragmentary character of modern existence – not to mention those movements in music, drama, art and architecture which, in the early part of the twentieth century, argued for the qualitative disintegration of the way in which people live.[6] Indeed, it was Canetti's great book *Crowds and Power*[7] which demonstrated, once and for all, the way in which the illusion of unity in society masks a greater issue, namely the existence and release of forces darker and more sinister, concealing the very nature which knowledge and understanding claim in the name of reason. In Britten's opera *Peter Grimes* one has a sobering illustration of this point, as the crowd leaving church in the second act translates seamlessly into the mob which will hound Grimes to his death. I do not say 'suicide', because the question remains whether Grimes genuinely takes his own life, or is in fact constructively murdered by the prejudices and citizenry of a community which marginalizes those who are simply different.[8]

All of these ideas are, of course, integral to Jesus of Nazareth's trial before Pontius Pilate, as related in John 18, culminating in the latter's question: 'What is truth?' (John 18.38). Within a context of institutional power and authority, that of the Roman State, it is axiomatic for the Fourth Gospel that Pilate's question receives no answer other than the personal existence of the Ascended Lord before him; Christ's heavenly status, the *truth* of which John writes, allows of no demonstration, solely the faith of those who are of the light.[9] The forces of darkness and mendacity, of which John speaks so eloquently yet tragically, are evidenced solely by the Word's silence; their simonical ways are marginalized to the extremes of the world and human existence, as was Judas Iscariot when confronted by the life of the Beloved Disciple (John 13.21–30). And as with the Fourth Gospel, so with so much of the Christian tradition: the absolute conviction of heteronomous truth has shaped and moulded, indeed has crushed the life out of, the way in which Christianity understands the contingency and variety of life and creation. With great gains there are often great losses, and so it is with the Johannine doctrine of the incarnation: certainty desiccates the fragmentary nature of the world in which people live.[10]

And yet Pilate's question, and, as importantly, the context in which it was articulated, when taken seriously, asks another, more fundamental question: in a situation dominated by crowds and power, as with Jesus' trial but now also in the world in which we live, does Christianity *really* suggest that God's relationship with the world is expressible solely as the silence of those who belong and thereby judge? Does the doctrine of the incarnation *really* argue that truth, for Christianity, is an absolute, closed to time and change? Or do the incarnation and ascension reveal and conceal a more fundamental claim, that God as the *mystery* of the world is the mystery of the *world*, and thereby present in a place of contingency and fragmentation? Finally, is it not of the sacramental essence of the Christian faith, that throughout time God incarnate and ascended acknowledges fragmentation as the constitutive principle of Being itself? This is to return to Schelling's world, and therefore to ours; but it is also to advance to the realm of systematic theology, the ancient stronghold of Christianity, but one today fallen perilously into Bunyan's 'slough of Despond'. The questions one must now ask as a matter of urgency – ontological, epistemological, and semantic – devolve responsibly upon one central issue, namely the good reasons present in Christian doctrine for rehabilitating Pontius Pilate, and thereby asking again today: 'What is truth?' Only by answering this question in and for our own historical context can we hope to speak of God in public *successfully*.

Of course, the task of rehabilitating Pilate has been attempted before, albeit implicitly: Friedrich Nietzsche confronted these same ideas in *Beyond Good and Evil*, and though Nietzsche himself wrote on behalf of Zarathustra, the teacher of the will to power and the eternal recurrence of the same – heavily reminiscent of the Christian doctrines of grace and eschatology – one can initially acknowledge his guidance.[11] For Nietzsche, Pilate's question is against truth; Pilate knows that he can receive no answer, because there is no such thing as truth *per se*. And, for Nietzsche, this is evidence of a greater insight, namely that there are no such general or universal principles *at all* to which people can appeal for power and authority. For Nietzsche, the absence of any such principles results in the death of God, as proclaimed in Zarathustra's Prologue; but it is a theme which receives more philosophical treatment in *Beyond Good and Evil*, Nietzsche's 'prologue to a philosophy of the future'.[12] Today, postmodernist thinkers appeal to Nietzsche as the first prophet of the end of all 'metanarratives', those attempts to formulate a general theory of everything which, philosophically, found their apotheosis in Hegel's *Phenomenology of Spirit*. Good, evil, God, knowledge, being, truth . . .: all are obsolete in a world of pure or thoroughgoing immanence, where contingency, limit and fragmentation govern chaotically all historical existence. Into this flux, Zarathustra announces a song of hope, one which leads to sincerity, but not responsibility for creation in any general sense.[13]

'Truth' for Nietzsche, consequently, is something premised not on the basis of general theory, but rather on a specific, individual life, indeed *each* individual life: as Harry Haller in Hesse's *Steppenwolf*, we are each confronted by the Magic Theatre of possibility; to enter, one must buy a ticket, and to buy a ticket, one must divest oneself of one's former existence.[14] Yes, Nietzsche, too, is all about repentance, conversion, *new creation*: but it is a story of *personal* re-creation, not an appeal to a divine *alter ego* from which people receive ready-made salvation. At bottom, Nietzsche is a good European liberal, standing in the same tradition as Rousseau's *Social Contract*, Kant's *Critique of Practical Reason* and Flaubert's *Sentimental Education*: self-education through encounters and relations with others is both the moral freedom *and* responsibility of each individual. Hence Nietzsche's parody of Hegel's philosophy, something finding explicit echoes in Musil's *The Man Without Qualities*, Mann's *Reflections of a Nonpolitical Man*, and Hesse's *The Glass Bead Game*.[15]

The point of Nietzsche's argument is therefore very simple: we are all thrown into a world of immanence and contingency, dominated by time and change, by what is transitory and illusory; and so we are all challenged individually to generate our own meaning, to make sense of our own world, for ourselves. Truth is thus historical: it, too, is subject to change and contingency; it, too, is transitory and illusory. Pilate's question, writes Nietzsche, does not allow of no demonstration; it allows of no *answer*. It is not axiomatic; it is *ironic*, and as such chimeric: like the Cheshire Cat it fades away, leaving behind solely the fading smile of an individual who knows that humanity is doomed as soon as it searches for its answers beyond the parameters of this limited, temporal world. Pilate gazed upon a beaten man, one who, in Schweitzer's memorable expression, threw himself upon the wheel of history, but was crushed by it; only, as we now know, argues Nietzsche, there is no such thing as the 'wheel' of history, solely the eternal recurrence of the same: that one wills one's own life so sincerely that, even if everything recurs eternally, one would not wish anything differently.

Within this rhetoric, Christianity generally finds only despair, that of anti-realism, in Don Cupitt's sense, of Matthew Arnold's 'sea of faith', ebbing slowly away, a beautiful image grown stale by endless repetition in recent British theology. At this point people start speaking of relativity, a situation in which the power and authority of Christianity fall away. Notions like limitation, contingency, immanence, so obviously juxtaposing apparently traditional religious motifs such as sovereignty, omnipotence and transcendence, challenge too many general preconceptions of God; they seem to marginalize that very divine glory which so much devotional and liturgical language seeks to convey and maintain. At the point where people want to bring God into the midst of their lives, where they attempt to domesticate God as positively as possible, notions like limitation, contingency and fragmentation simply do not signal meaningfully. Nietzsche's critique is rejected *a priori* simply linguistically by church communities which need to affirm before they can deny, say 'Yes' before they can say 'No'. This much is confirmed by even a cursory examination of the rise of fundamentalism in Christianity since the 1970s, a phenomenon not limited solely to this religion.[16]

What one finds in so much popular devotion therefore is a rejection of the circumstances of Jesus' own agony, trial, and death, in favour of an affirmation of the perceived supernatural qualities of the Risen and Ascended Christ. This is clearly the Fourth Gospel's intention, which is why Jesus need not answer Pilate's question; but that intention has been translated into a more general

Christian sensibility; i.e. that the *completeness* of God's presence as Christ supersedes any question of the *incompleteness* of God's historical revelation;[17] that from the perspective of divine power — which of course the Church now possesses and wields — matters like darkness, loss and exploitation are themselves marginalized out of all relationship. The Fourth Gospel is therefore the Holy Scripture of the Ascended Lord, a singular text for a singular event.

There are two problems with the Johannine understanding of God as the mystery of the world, however, problems so great and weighty that they threaten to compromise the very integrity of the text. The first is epistemological; i.e. it has to do with how one knows of God in Jesus Christ. The second is metaphysical, and has to do with how one interprets and understands the relationship between time and eternity. Both are central to the constructive retrieval of doctrine which I am attempting in this chapter.

Epistemology is about the good reasons one has to claim that one knows certain things; so that for Christianity the good reasons for its knowledge of God are derived from the story of Jesus, and are hence traditional and biblical. More importantly, however, what one claims to know of God in Jesus Christ is limited by the specific circumstances of Jesus' mission and message, his life on earth. In Mark's Gospel, and Paul's letters, this limitation is expressed via a profound appreciation of eschatology — the last things — and the conviction that what was begun in Jesus Christ is yet *incomplete* in his earthly life; that Christ will return to consummate God's power and authority on earth. Hence one can speak of the general *linear progression* of this reasoning in Mark and Paul: the revelation of God's will in Jesus Christ moves dynamically towards resolution at an indexed moment of future time. This theology is teleological.

In the Fourth Gospel, by contrast, one is nowhere presented with an *incomplete* story, but rather a complete narrative of God's completed action; indeed, John's Prologue expounds all of the central points of a complete understanding of God's will — complete, because the Johannine community is that of the presence of God, a claim validated for faith by Christ's sending of the Holy Spirit or Counsellor. There is no sense in the Fourth Gospel therefore of teleology, of linear progression towards a future goal, of the incompleteness of present action. Rather, time is circular: Christ moves seamlessly from incarnation to ascension, at each stage revealing by his sheer presence that God has come to the world, and that the world — or at least, a small part of it — has returned to God. Every sign, saying, encounter and action of Jesus simply confirms the inevitability of this revelation as a completed event, so that at the climax of Jesus' life on earth, all he need say is: 'It is finished.' John even provides a narrative *within* Jesus' ministry — the raising of Lazarus – to demonstrate that Jesus' *complete* power and authority are unconstrained by any imaginable, historical circumstance. For those who believe even though they have not seen, some things simply do not need to wait until after Jesus' resurrection, but are evident throughout his life.

One of the beauties of the Fourth Gospel is that nothing is left to chance; one has the strongest possible impression that John has measured every single word, that *every* clause and proposition carries full weight and meaning. Thus when one reads, in John 18.36, that Jesus' kingdom is not of this world, and that the Father will not send force to act in this world on behalf of the Son, one can only take seriously John's theology. The Fourth Gospel is about distinction and separation; of the difference between that which is God's, and that which is of the world. For John, there *are* no epistemological difficulties associated with distinguishing between these two states, because they are identified by God's complete action in Jesus Christ. All one requires, consequently, is the correct ontological 'information' regarding the Son's being and power – which the Fourth Gospel duly provides. The incarnation in the Fourth Gospel, consequently, is all about the power of completion, not incompletion, so that one is reminded of Eliot's line from *Four Quartets*, 'In my end is my beginning'.[18]

These epistemological moves in the Fourth Gospel have certain important metaphysical implications, pivoting upon the central notions of completeness and circularity. The Son's descent into and ascent from the world – see John 1.51 – is both a temporal and an eternal event; i.e. it is meaningful and constitutive for John of both realms, this world and beyond. But this itself means that the incarnation and ascension, as one complete and circular event, says something about both human and divine being. It says that this is how God comes to the world and the world to God, certainly; but it also says that this movement or relationship is symbiotic, and therefore about how God and the world actually *are*. God's complete action in Jesus Christ thus says something complete, and hence ontological, about the way in which God knows the world as Jesus Christ – a knowledge which is perfect as presence and revelation. God comes to the world completely as Jesus Christ, which means that God knows time – eternally – through the specific time of Jesus Christ; i.e. the temporal duration of his life on earth. Moreover, because that life is complete and circular, it follows for John that humanity knows God *only* as Jesus Christ, so that for the Fourth Gospel one can say that God is in eternity *as* God is in time as Jesus Christ.[19]

What does all of this mean? One can answer this if one considers the tantalizing question: 'What happens to the body of Christ after the ascension?'[20] The temptation is to attempt to answer this spatially; i.e. by describing an alternative realm – Heaven – in which is *located* the body of Jesus as the second person of the Trinity; a solution which found currency for many centuries of the Christian tradition. From an understanding of John's metaphysics of time and eternity, however, one recognizes that this question can in fact only receive a *temporal* answer. Thus, the answer to the question: 'Where is Jesus' body now?' can only be: '2,000 years ago in Palestine.' Or, more precisely and cogently: 'Time – the body of Jesus – is eternally present in God, because the historical person of Jesus Christ as Word is *eternally* present in time 2,000 years ago in Palestine.' John thereby has it both ways: God is always present as Jesus of Nazareth – giving signs, performing miracles, dying and rising – because, as Ascended Son, Jesus Christ simply *is* always. It is an argument about being and time, not space and locale.

This is all utterly ingenious, and to the best of my ability I have to say that the Fourth Gospel is correct as far as its metaphysics of time and eternity is concerned. Problems arise, however, when one asks the question: 'What status does John give to this relationship between time and eternity in Jesus Christ?' Clearly, for John, the claims being made here are *realist*; this is the way in which God *really* relates to the world, so that Pilate's question *really* receives the personal answer of the Risen and Ascended Lord.[21] This is where I want to argue that John went wrong, and where the later Chalcedonian Definition reaffirmed a correct understanding of the incarnation and ascension.[22]

As I have argued, John is writing for a community which is concerned with certainty: certainty that God has acted decisively in a specific individual, certainty that God is present within the Johannine community sacramentally and as Counsellor. John therefore articulates a *theological* epistemology, founded upon the conviction that God's revelation is complete because God is completely present as Jesus Christ. Thus power and authority in the Fourth Gospel have to do with a Jesus Christ who is Risen and Ascended, and thereby distinguished from the world even as he is in the world. And hence worldly power and authority, in the guise of Pontius Pilate, entirely misunderstand the true nature and character of the individual as whom God is present. Pontius Pilate is simply wrong, because the world is simply wrong.

Rehabilitating Pontius Pilate, however, is not simply a consequence of taking seriously Nietzsche's arguments about power and authority in the world; it is also a consequence of taking seriously Chalcedon's understanding of the incarnation and ascension as *analogical* talk about God's presence in the world as Jesus Christ, whereby 'analogy' is defined as 'reasoning from approximately parallel cases'.[23] Analogically, as opposed to 'really', John's metaphysics of time and eternity still makes a claim about Jesus Christ's person; but it does so whilst acknowledging that the language employed to articulate that claim is approximately parallel, and so incomplete. Understanding the incarnation and ascension analogically, rather than realistically, acknowledges the important epistemological criticism that all human knowledge is inherently incomplete, and therefore contingent upon the way in which power and authority function *in the world*. Without this stricture, incarnation and ascension are about divine manipulation, rather than the expression of divine love *as* acceptance of limitation, contingency, and fragmentation for the sake of the world.

I can illustrate the importance of this argument by reference to three central doctrines of the Christian faith, namely cross, resurrection and eucharist. First, Jesus' crucifixion is the acceptance by God incarnate of the final limitation placed upon humanity, death itself. By accepting death into the Godhead, the Son affirms the Father's will to identify with the fullest limitations of creation. Second, the resurrection of the Son by the Father, in the power of the Holy Spirit, is the affirmation of God's triumph over death, but a triumph which is not so much the negation of death as its eschatological consummation. It is in this sense that one's understanding of, and faith in, Jesus' resurrection are still important, because one's knowledge of resurrection is conditioned by the 'not yet' quality of the fullness of the Last Judgement, albeit proleptically revealed in Jesus Christ as first fruits. Third, and most graphically, the eucharist is the sacramental and therefore incomplete mediation of God's willingness to be fragmented, torn apart on the cross, for the sake of humanity. Analogically, the fate of the Son in being so shattered speaks loudly to our own understanding of all those so fragmented by the character and difficulty of human life, be they oppressed socially, exploited economically, or tragically handicapped by nature.[24]

These three points will be largely obvious, resting as they do upon a straightforward interpretation of God's *kenosis* or self-emptying as incarnate Son. The Fourth Gospel, however, makes one realize that this *kenosis* cannot be limited solely to the cross, because the cross is simply one part of a completed event of incarnation and ascension. Every event and action of Jesus' life on earth between incarnation and ascension reveals God's self-emptying presence, from the smallest through to the greatest of Jesus' activities. Thus Christology – interpretation of the manifold doctrines of Christ – cannot be restricted solely to certain key moments in Jesus' life, because that *entire* life was one key moment, indeed the eternally revealed and concealed key moment, within which all humanity shares in eternity, and all divinity shares in time. To this extent, consequently, Bultmann's notion of the eternal moment of encounter between God and humanity in Christ, and so the eternal moment of decision for humanity, is correct; but only in the same way that Nietzsche's understanding of the eternal recurrence of the same, through which all willed existence must figuratively pass, is correct. The point, finally, is that Nietzsche, like Christianity, wants to make truth claims on the basis of what it is to speak positively and negatively of completeness and incompleteness by analogy with the contingent circumstances of historical existence (though with very different conclusions, of course). For both Nietzsche and Christianity, this is essential to their ability to speak *publicly*.

Bringing the argument back to Nietzsche is an important move at this point. As I stated earlier, Nietzsche's two major doctrines are the eternal recurrence of the same and the will to power. The former is extensively developed in *Thus Spoke Zarathustra*, and bears significant comparison with Christianity's notion of eschatology, as I have said; but the latter is more difficult to pin down: it finds only short treatment in *Thus Spoke Zarathustra*, and subsequently receives brutal editing in the fragments and commentary published by Nietzsche's sister. In fact, one is almost justified in speaking of a 'pathology' of will to power commentary and transmission, in which Nietzsche's most difficult ideas are absorbed within an ideology of violence and domination. The worst example of this was Nietzsche's 'translation' into National Socialist currency during the years 1933–45.

By relating the will to power to Christianity's understanding of *grace*, however, I hope to illuminate some important qualities in Nietzsche's thought, which will inform what I want to go on and say about how one speaks publicly of Christian truth claims in contemporary society and culture. My emphasis here is upon the understanding of power itself, why it is fundamental to any interpretation of human existence, and how it relates to Christianity's own public self-definition as a true religion.

Nietzsche condemns all general theories and principles, arguing instead for the contingency and fragmentation of the modern world, and the isolation of the individual within it. It therefore follows, if Nietzsche is consistent, that the will to power, like the eternal recurrence of the same, cannot be such a general theory or principle. Rather, it must be something different for each individual, so that each in his or her specific context exercises his or her own will to power to realize the best possibilities of his or her life. Hence, the will to power is the ability both to suppress one's former existence, thereby 'shedding' the debris of inauthenticity which shrouds and impedes one's genuine humanity, and to realize that genuine humanity, which is itself integral to each and every human nature. That this will be achieved by very few, Nietzsche readily acknowledges; he is a true educator, and knows that the level of reflection he requires is seldom realized. But *that* it is possible . . . this much one can write of creatively and meaningfully, though it reaches the literally fantastic form of *Thus Spoke Zarathustra*.

Comparisons with modern literature are informative at this juncture. In Thomas Mann's *The Magic Mountain*, Hans Castorp confronts such existential possibilities on the eponymous mountain, though generally within the confines of his sanatorium; but it is unclear precisely what status Mann wants to give to the 'magic' quality of Castorp's experiences. The same thing can be said of the Magic Theatre in Hesse's *Steppenwolf*: is it mental? emotional? logical? existential? Again, the precise status is indeterminate. In Musil's *The Man Without Qualities*, it does at least seem readily apparent that Ulrich's existence is measured by the parameters of the Habsburg empire and its endless bureaucracy; but, as Kafka's work makes clear in both *The Trial* and *The Castle*, defining the level upon which such parabolic works operate is almost impossible. Notwithstanding Georg Lukacs' wry comment upon being dragged away by the KGB in Hungary in 1956 – 'I was wrong; Kafka *was* a realist' – literary modernism – and one can add here Continental writers like Broch, Canetti and Kundera, as well as English-speakers like Eliot and Pound, the unique world of Joyce, and more recent South Americans such as Gabriel García Márquez and Mario Vargas Llosa – has found it almost impossible to give any precision to that potential or agency within a literary world which might equate with Nietzsche's will to power. And, of course, in art and music, where the attempts to find new media and languages – cubism, dada, serialism – are that much more apparent, we recognize the same point again and again: modernity is about fragmentation and individualization, even in questions of motive force.

At first glance, Christian theology would seem to escape this situation at a single bound. Granted the difficulties in modern literature, art, music and philosophy, there is something inherently 'unmodern' about modern theology: or, better, *pre*modern; i.e. a status given *a priori* to the stresses and faults highlighted in Nietzsche's work. As Barth repeatedly argued, Christianity is all about *eschatological realism*; it is all about something really 'out there' coming really 'in here', so that all ontological, epistemological and semantic questions themselves begin axiomatically, and therefore non-critically, in certain very specific, fideistic circumstances. For Barth the problems of Kafka and Canetti are simply secular concerns; they have little or no bearing upon the real business of Christian theology. For Barth, consequently, grace – God's own will to power – is a real presence, creating eschatologically the conditions necessary for the proclamation of the kingdom, with Jesus, for the life of faith in the body of Christ, in the Church, and for salvation to occur, in eternity. Interestingly, a similar understanding of 'real presence' underpins

George Steiner's book *Real Presences*, from the late 1980s, arguing somewhat inconclusively for the role of grace in artistic creation. Steiner's claim might be correct, of course; but *demonstrating* it will prove impossible epistemologically.[25]

Importantly, if one asks the name of the power which makes grace grace, eschatology eschatology, and God's power in the world God's power in the world, then from the New Testament one receives a very straightforward answer: God's Spirit, the Holy Spirit, the Counsellor of the Fourth Gospel. Thus it is God's own power and authority as Spirit in the world which empowers Jesus of Nazareth to perform healings and miracles, to teach in parables, and to proclaim the kingdom of God; it is the Holy Spirit who is with Jesus on the cross, thereby making of those wood and nails an eschatological event; it is the Holy Spirit in whose power Jesus is raised and, consequently, ascends; and it is the Holy Spirit who is, subsequently, poured out upon the Church in Acts 2, whence to be God's real presence in the world. Without this Holy Spirit, the story of Jesus Christ would not be the story of God's re-creative action through incarnation and ascension; for it is the presence of the Holy Spirit, finally, which makes revelation *revelation*.

Apparently there is a tension here between the powerful foundations of Christian self-understanding in the Holy Spirit, and the treatment of power in terms of contingency and fragmentation one finds in Nietzsche and modernist literature; but on anything more than cursory examination this is not the case. That the Holy Spirit, as God's eschatological motor, is absolute, is of course axiomatic for Christian faith; but it is by no means clear that the way in which Jesus wields the Holy Spirit's power occurs absolutely. On the contrary, the New Testament is full of incidents of conflict between Jesus' power and evil spirits; Jesus' crucifixion is itself a conflictual event; and the subsequent history of the early Church in Acts is similarly compromised by the circumstances in which the apostles at times found themselves. One has only to think of Paul's speech on the Areopagus in Acts 17 to realize that the Church's early mission was not characterized by unremitting success.

Historical circumstance in and of itself, however, is insufficient to sustain a genuinely systematic theological argument; one requires doctrinally good reasons to sustain a specific position, certainly when it involves, as mine does, a large degree of qualification of traditional Christian self-understanding. For example: granted that Jesus' activities in the power of the Holy Spirit, and subsequently the apostles', are compromised by the contingency and fragmentation of power in the world, a situation one can rationalize doctrinally by appealing to the kenotic character of incarnation and ascension; is this yet sufficient to speak of the degree of qualification and sheer mess that one finds in Nietzsche and Musil? Given that Jesus' trial before Pilate has certain apparently Kafkaesque qualities; what good reasons does one have for making a yet stronger correlation between the modern predicament and Christian doctrine? Incarnation and ascension: yes, these affirm throughout the story of Jesus and Christianity that God's will is constantly tested in a power struggle with the world, in which social and cultural contingency play a large part; but does this give one the right to qualify Christian truth claims as one dares to speak of God in public?

The answer to these questions must be 'Yes and No': or, better: yes, in the name of contextual interpretation in modernity, one must acknowledge modernity's own predicament; but no, I have not yet said enough to establish doctrinally the force of my argument. There must be more explicitly *doctrinal* interpretation, before the full force of my argument can be elaborated. To achieve this I want to make a systematic move which is easily overlooked these days, particularly when interpreting the Christological doctrines of incarnation through ascension.

Incarnation and ascension cannot be understood properly if they are regarded as *binitarian* events, as functions of the relationship between the Father and the Son. Rather, systematic theology requires the doctrine of the Trinity to make sense of incarnation and ascension. Why? Because incarnation and ascension are only eschatological events in the presence of the Holy Spirit; it is the return/sending of the Spirit which validates Jesus' mission and message. Thus, everything which happens to Jesus Christ between incarnation and ascension is a function of the relationships between *three* persons: Father, Son, and Holy Spirit.[26]

Why does this require the doctrine of the Trinity *per se*, rather than a notional God acting through worldly persons and events? Because the power of the Spirit is the qualitatively equal presence of God in the world, rather than a subordinate operation. Christian faith maintains, via its understanding of eschatology, that the presence of God as Creator, Redeemer and Counsellor is always the *same* presence — an axiom equally relevant whether one is speaking of Galilee, Golgotha or Pentecost. This is the meaning of grace: that whether revealed in Creation, as incarnate Son, or as gifts of the Spirit, it is always equally the presence *of God* and therefore of three persons eternally one in a will revealed and concealed economically in time.[27]

This has profound implications for the way in which systematic theology understands the doctrine of the Holy Spirit, something traditionally neglected in Western theology, but without which the incarnation and ascension makes no sense. Concisely, the key issue here concerns the work of the Holy Spirit: is it simply to enable and, subsequently, to endorse the Son's achievements? Is it subservient to whatever occurs in the interplay of wills between the Father and the Son, as revealed in the garden of Gethsemane? Or does the Holy Spirit have its own specific agenda, something which is of equal importance to the Son's incarnation, though it only becomes revealed in the light of the Son's incarnation and ascension? The answer is the latter, for one very important reason.[28]

The key here is provided by the Fourth Gospel, specifically John 16.12–13. Jesus is conducting the farewell discourse, instructing the disciples and thereby the putative Church, saying at this point: 'I have yet many things to say to you, but you cannot bear them now. When the Spirit of truth comes, he will guide you into all the truth. . .' It is only one verse, but it contains an argument of paramount importance for everything one can say today about Christian self-definition. Jesus Christ is saying that *not everything* has been revealed through incarnation and ascension; *more* will be revealed after Pentecost, after the Holy Spirit has been sent to the Church. Certainly, I have no doubt at all that John intends this to be a self-validating argument for the Johannine community, so that it believes itself gnoseologically to be a unique institution; but, more generally, systematic theology can recognize the argument as central to the doctrine of the Holy Spirit. The claim here is simple: after incarnation and ascension, more will be revealed *by the Holy Spirit*; revelation continues *in the power of the Holy Spirit*; the Holy Spirit in, by, and through the Church *has its own task*: to lead people further into the truth. The implication here is enormous: the work of revelation continues after incarnation and ascension; the revelation of truth, and, consequently, Christian knowledge and understanding of truth, is *incomplete*. That the work of the Holy Spirit is genuinely and equally the work of God, and therefore completely identical as willed event with incarnation and ascension – and indeed creation – is vouchsafed by the doctrine of the Trinity. Nevertheless, Christianity lives in and *towards* that power of the Holy Spirit which is in the process of carrying people further into truth. This is not teleology, that movement towards a specific goal which characterized Marcan and Pauline eschatology; it is *protology*, the gradual unfolding historically of something *a priori* to the contingent and fragmentary *locus* of revelation – the governing principle of Schelling's philosophy of revelation in 1841.[29]

One cannot debase this insight by claiming that it functions solely within the confines of Christian uniqueness; that would be to ignore a fundamental implication of this theological argument. The economy here is signal: as the Holy Spirit empowered Jesus Christ to go out into the world to do God's will, so the Holy Spirit empowers the Church – the body of the Ascended Lord – to go out into the world to do God's will. 'Doing God's will' is hence a matter of encountering the world, its societies, cultures, contingencies and fragmentations, but always acknowledging, on the basis of the very *heart* of Christian doctrine, that the truth Christianity claims and proclaims is not yet complete; that no matter how loud and long one proclaims the incarnation and ascension, as long as the world lives there is yet more truth to be revealed. Christianity has neither the power nor the authority to govern creation absolutely, nor to know God's will completely, nor to prescribe the ways in which people might encounter God, nor, finally, to say what is *the truth*. Pontius Pilate is thereby rehabilitated not in spite of his worldliness – something irredeemable in the Fourth Gospel – but *because of it*; for in that worldliness, as Nietzsche implicitly realized, there is the possibility of truth, and therefore God. Thus is creation, in all its variety and future potential, writ large upon the imaginations of people everywhere.

As I come towards the end of this chapter, I am reminded of Montgomery's opening remarks to the troops on the eve of the battle of El Alamein: 'As God once said, and I think rightly . . .'; but it is not my place or intention to call into question the way in which people believe in God. For better or for worse I am a catholic systematic theologian; I occupy, however inadequately, an old office between historical and practical theologies, practising a theoretical discipline. I look at certain problems in order to address certain issues; but how, and to what extent, those issues can be resolved is the job of belief in its entirety. That said, I want to end by identifying three areas where I think rehabilitating Pontius Pilate can have important effects.

First, that truth is incomplete in the world means that there is no perspective from which I, as a Christian theologian, can claim to know and understand the truth *per se*; and hence there is no perspective from which I can claim that other religions are either invalid or non-promissory of salvation. On the contrary, and axiomatically, if the Spirit of God is leading people ever further into the truth, and if this is a function of God's eternal will to be revealed in the world, then it is clear to me that God speaks and saves through more media than those named via incarnation and ascension. That I am a Christian theologian means I speak of the Ascended Lord; but the gift of the Holy Spirit *by* the Ascended Lord means I can speak solely of what I imperfectly know, rather than of what I prejudge others to know and believe.

Second, and limiting my words here to the two catholic churches to which I am drawn: the fact that the Holy Spirit is leading us ever further into truth means that we must embrace that which is new and different within our own limited and contingent understanding of God's sacramental mediation. Nowhere is this clearer than in the currently vexed question of the ordination of priests, and the canard of gender-specific sexuality which presently dominates so much conversation. I say quite clearly that as the Holy Spirit today is the same power which validates eternally the full humanity of the Son, so humanity in all of its diversity mediates sacramentally the meaning of incarnation and ascension. In Christ there is neither male nor female, nor homosexual, nor bisexual, nor heterosexual, nor able-bodied, nor handicapped, nor black, nor white. Even as I speak, as Christians believe and witness, Jesus Christ walks abroad preaching good news to everyone, in the power of the same Spirit which today leads people ever further into the truth. That is the sole theological basis for identifying Christ with anyone, within or without the Church.

Third, there is no one answer to the problem of evil; though I profess Christ as salvation, therefore, there are things today for which that revelation of the truth cannot prepare us, and for which we must pray and hope for future understanding. It is one year to the day since the discovery of James Bulger's body in Liverpool, murdered by two ten-year-old boys.[30] All will recall the spiritual void into which those events cast the nation; probably most of us present attempted then, and subsequently, to articulate *some* understanding of unthinkable evil, as others have attempted to understand other, equally unthinkable, evils like the Armenian and Jewish holocausts, Northern Ireland and Bosnia. Everyone will and must seek to understand in their own way; and for Christian theology this will always mean in terms of the incarnation and ascension of the Son. But, equally, we must hope and believe that the power of the Spirit can and will lead us out of darkness, evil and suffering, towards a deeper truth. I do not expect a utopian resolution of the shattered world in which people live their lives; but I do believe that 'God is in the details' is a spiritual reality which holds tremendous potential for how one understands the presence of God, as One who comes to specific situations, and particular individuals and communities.

How to end, then?[31] I can think of no better way than to appeal to the words of Jon Sobrino, writing of the murder and martyrdom of the Salvadorean Jesuits in 1989, believing that my own 'portrait of the theologian as a young man' cannot but be improved by listening to the words of a theologian who daily confronts far greater difficulties than I can imagine, in order to address the Christian faith to an audience desperately in need of the gospel. If they are good enough for Christians in El Salvador, they are certainly good enough for me:

> It is not easy to know how to keep on hoping and we must all answer this question in our own way. It seems that everything is against hope, but for me at least, where I see there has been great love, I see hope being

born again. This is not a rational conclusion and perhaps not even theological. It is simply true . . .

Amen.

Notes

1. F. W. J. Schelling, *Philosophie der Offenbarung*, ed. Manfred Frank (Frankfurt a.M., 1977), p. 89. Schelling's work, and its relevance for Christian theology, has been woefully neglected; but cf. Andrew Bowie, *Schelling and Modern European Philosophy: An Introduction* (London, 1993).
2. On Bultmann and Heidegger, cf. my book *Bultmann: Towards a Critical Theology* (Cambridge, 1991), particularly ch. 3; on Moltmann and Bloch, cf. Richard Bauckham, *Moltmann: Messianic Theology in the Making* (Basingstoke, 1987); on Pannenberg, cf. his most recent discussion of this question in his *Systematic Theology* 1 (Edinburgh, 1991), pp. 1–61. On the Christological implications of process theology's understanding of truth, cf. Schubert Ogden, *The Point of Christology* (London, 1982).
3. On this question I am particularly influenced by Jean-Pierre Jossua, *The Condition of the Witness* (London, 1985); see specifically ch. 5, on 'Relations between believers and non-Christians', as background for my own argument.
4. On this question in Hegel, cf. Jürgen Habermas, *Knowledge and Human Interests* (Cambridge, 1987), pp. 25–42.
5. Francis Fukuyama, *The End of History and the Last Man* (London, 1992).
6. Robert Musil, *The Man Without Qualities* (4 vols, London, 1979–); Marcel Proust, *Remembrance of Things Past* (3 vols, London, 1981–); Thomas Mann, *The Magic Mountain* (London, 1979); Hermann Hesse, *The Glass Bead Game* (London, 1972); T. S. Eliot, 'The Waste Land' in *Collected Poems 1909–1962* (London, 1963), pp. 61–86; Elias Canetti, *Auto da Fe* (London, 1978). In terms of other aesthetic movements, obvious examples would be serialism in music (or the Second Viennese School more generally), dadaism and cubism in art, and the Bauhaus in architecture.
7. Elias Canetti, *Crowds and Power* (Harmondsworth, 1973).
8. My point here is an obvious one, and I claim no originality for it; cf. Philip Brett (compiler), *Benjamin Britten's Peter Grimes* (Cambridge, 1983), for a deeper treatment of Britten's opera.
9. On this question in the Fourth Gospel, cf. John Ashton, *Understanding the Fourth Gospel* (Oxford, 1991), pp. 205–37; and Thomas Brodie, *The Gospel According to John: A Literary and Theological Commentary* (Oxford, 1993), pp. 65–6.
10. Cf. Donald MacKinnon, 'On the relationship between the Trinity and Incarnation' in *Themes in Theology: The Three-fold Cord: Essays in Philosophy, Politics, and Theology* (Edinburgh, 1987).
11. On this question, cf. R. J. Hollingdale's introduction to *Thus Spoke Zarathustra* (London, 1969), pp. 25–6. On 'the will to power', cf. Maudemarie Clark, *Nietzsche on Truth and Philosophy* (Cambridge, 1990), pp. 205–44; on 'the eternal recurrence of the same' – *the* Nietzschean idea for modern theology – cf. Martin Heidegger, *Nietzsche II: The Eternal Recurrence of the Same* (San Francisco, 1984). On Nietzsche in general, I have found the following texts invaluable: Tracy B. Strong, *Friedrich Nietzsche and the Politics of Transfiguration* (expanded edn, Berkeley, CA, 1988); Alexander Nehamas, *Nietzsche: Life as Literature* (Cambridge, MA, 1985). I am indebted to discussions with Steven Else on this aspect of Nietzsche's thought.
12. Friedrich Nietzsche, *Beyond Good and Evil* (New York, 1966).

13. Cf. Allan Megill, *Prophets of Extremity: Nietzsche, Heidegger, Foucault, Derrida* (Berkeley, CA, 1985), pp. 29–102.
14. Hermann Hesse, *Steppenwolf* (London, 1965). On Hesse and Bultmann, cf. my article 'The play of a delicate shadow: Bultmann and Hesse in the Magic Theatre', *Literature and Theology* 2/1 (March 1988), pp. 96–111. On the notion of 'the Magic Theatre' in modern aesthetics, cf. George Pattison, *Kierkegaard: The Aesthetic and the Religious. From the Magic Theatre to the Crucifixion of the Image* (Basingstoke, 1992), in particular pp. 95–124.
15. Thomas Mann, *Reflections of a Nonpolitical Man* (New York, 1983). I would not want to make this point into anything more than a *general* theory here; but the collapse of revelation into pedagogics is, I would argue, fundamental to everything happening in *modern* theology from Kant onwards.
16. On which question cf. Gilles Kepel's recent study *The Revenge of God: The Resurgence of Islam, Christianity, and Judaism in the Modern World* (Cambridge, 1993).
17. I have developed this argument at greater length in my book *Critical Theology: Questions of Truth and Method* (Cambridge, 1994).
18. Eliot, 'Four Quartets' in op. cit., p. 204. Of course, it is not incidental that those words were written *after* Eliot's conversion to a thoroughly catholic and incarnational form of Anglicanism.
19. This much would seem to be axiomatic for Barth's mature theology.
20. The following discussion of this question is heavily dependent upon Ralph Norman's original research; my thanks to him for many valuable conversations about the ascension.
21. I am influenced here by Ingolf Dalferth's marvellous essay 'Karl Barth as eschatological realist' in S. W. Sykes (ed.), *Karl Barth: Centenary Essays* (Cambridge, 1989).
22. In what follows I will be reacting against John Hick's criticism of Chalcedon, particularly its so-called 'metaphorical' quality; cf. John Hick, *The Metaphor of God Incarnate* (London, 1993).
23. This much has been beautifully expressed in Karl Rahner's essay 'Current problems in Christology' in *Theological Investigations* 1 (London, 1961).
24. This is how Moltmann writes of the *therapeutic* quality of contemporary theology in *The Crucified God* (London, 1974).
25. George Steiner, *Real Presences* (London, 1989).
26. Moltmann has acknowledged this point in his recent book *The Spirit of Life: A Universal Affirmation* (London, 1992), though he does not develop it sufficiently.
27. The Orthodox tradition has a far more developed understanding of the person and work of the Holy Spirit, as is well known, and I have learned much here from reading works by Orthodox theologians such as Kallistos Ware and John Zizioulas.
28. Cf. Timothy (Kallistos) Ware, *The Orthodox Church* (London, 1964), pp. 234–6.
29. This does *not* mean that life lived towards the Holy Spirit, the gradual unfolding of revelation in history, equates to a spurious 'Whig theory of history'; my earlier emphasis upon the fragmentary nature of human existence militates against such a seamless interpretation of one's context. Truth cannot be limited within process; rather, *processional* interpretation is but one analogy for understanding revelation and grace within space and time.
30. This chapter was originally given as a lecture on 14 February 1994.
31. This last paragraph is taken from the conclusion to my book *Critical Theology: Questions of Truth and Method* (Cambridge, 1994).

10
'A time for silence' Dare we mention prayer?

Frances Young

More than once since I became Head of the Department of Theology, colleagues from elsewhere in the University have suggested that I have a 'hot line to the Almighty'. A recent opinion poll on belief in Britain included questions about experiencing or not experiencing answers to prayer. The presupposition behind such teasing and questions is that the power of prayer can be proved or disproved by empirical testing, that believers are chiefly interested in bending things in their own interest, and that this is all slightly ridiculous since, even if there is a God, which is doubtful, it is hardly likely that the universe will be governed in the interests of certain puny, self-centred individuals.

In such a context, it surely seems a 'time for silence', a time to cherish one's beliefs in private and avoid ridicule. We get the feeling that most people in our culture either identify with *Waiting for Godot*, the famous play of Samuel Beckett which depicts two characters vainly expecting someone to turn up, or, sure they are alone in the universe, have long since stopped waiting. For some others, the poet R. S. Thomas voices their sense of absence:

> Why no! I never thought other than
> That God is that great absence
> In our lives, the empty silence
> Within, the place where we go
> Seeking, not in hope to
> Arrive or find . . .[1]

The implicit ideology of the secular university campus led my predecessor in the Edward Cadbury Chair of Theology to insist that on no account should we be seen to form 'holy huddles'.[2] Theological colleges, Bible institutes, seminaries – they might start lectures and committees with prayer, but not a university department. For, as Hugh McLeod showed,[3] religion is no longer taken seriously with respect to 'public affairs'. When science has shown the absurdity of praying for rain, and common sense the impropriety of assuming that God is 'on *our* side' in situations of conflict and war, prayer seems no longer to belong to the so-called 'real world'.

On the whole, then, God and the churches are marginalized. Yet God is more often mentioned in public prayer than in any other form of public discourse. Many rites survive: prayers daily in the House of Commons and other public institutions, graces at formal dinners, civic services, regular broadcast services of worship, 'rites of passage' at marriages and funerals. Even universities countenance prayer on certain public occasions, such as a graduation service, or an annual service opening the session; here (in the University of Birmingham) there is a popular carol service. Many people presumably treat such rituals as duties to be endured, or folk celebrations full of nostalgia, and would deny believing participation. There is a gap between public and private stance.

But the gap often works the other way. For despite public scepticism, polls suggest that a surprising number of people who take no active part in regular religious activity continue to claim that they believe in God and pray in private, often not just intermittently but regularly. Furthermore, there is the paradoxical fact that, in this post-Christian secularized age, there is a burgeoning interest in spirituality, often vague and amorphous, yet a significant reaction against materialism, technology, the dominance of scientific medicine and so on. What seems to have happened is a disjunction between private and public prayer, coupled with a certain embarrassment about it.

Of course, the *subject* of prayer is not alien to the university. Critical analysis of any human activity is part of a university's mission. So prayer and religious rites have long been important in fields such as anthropology, sociology, and psychology. In a programme of theology or religious studies, the nature of religious activity, of which prayer is clearly a central feature, would necessarily have a place, and would draw upon the methodologies of such human sciences, along with study of the history of ritual, and comparative analysis of the public and private prayers and rites of different religious groups. There would be an attempt at objective assessment, from the position of external observer. So, we dare mention prayer, it seems, as long as we are engaged in the second-order activity of analysis and external observation.

What I want to do in this chapter is to consider whether we can go further.

Might it, perhaps, be the case that, alongside observation and critique of such religious activity, a rounded theology requires the discourse of prayer? Might prayer be a good test case for analysis and assessment of particular theological positions? Could prayer be, after all, the *locus* of an important intersection between public and private worlds, integrating individuals into community, and shattering the limitations of domestic, or even sectional, horizons? Maybe we shall find that, while there is indeed a time to keep silence, there is also a time to speak.[4]

Perspectives from the past

The empiricist tease, I suggest, shows little appreciation of the nature of prayer, and parallels rationalist discussions which began with the rise of Greek philosophy 2,500 years ago. To take that kind of long perspective has always seemed to me to be important. The past may well be a foreign country,[5] but to travel abroad is to modify one's view of things. In this chapter we shall comment on our present by 'passing over' to other periods and places.

There are reasons to be encouraged in this approach. Throughout a good deal of my life, the drive of modernity has tended to devalue the past, as well as 'unmodernized' cultures of the present, a notion of progress being implicit which assumed we moderns knew best. Now, it seems, we are in a post-modern world, which, in the realm of architecture at least, is rediscovering the wisdom of classical forms – even traditional materials, like brick. For all the differences, there are now intriguing parallels with the Graeco-Roman world – with its movement of peoples; its enlarged horizons; its loss of local, ethnocentric communities in a unifying amalgam of cultural and religious identities; its feeling that ideas and customs from the East had a certain exotic flavour, and that all religions are ultimately the same – though the duty of public conformity despite private scepticism expressed by some Roman authors was perhaps more characteristic of the Victorian age than our own.[6]

As it happens, my apprentice work as a scholar was devoted to exploring the meaning of sacrifice in the religiously pluralist world of antiquity – in particular, the way in which the early Christians radically shifted the reference of such language while sharing the assumptions around them.[7] Relevant observations arising from that research include the inseparability of sacrifice and prayer, and the significance of the kind of critical evaluation of religious practices that went on in the ancient world.

We tend to associate the term sacrifice with the slaughtering of animals in a ritual context; but in the ancient world, prayers were almost invariably accompanied by material gifts of some sort – the first-fruits of the crop, wine, honey, flour, money, workmen's tools, statuettes, clothing and jewellery and so on. Making such offerings was normal practice for all the various tribes and nations which eventually made up the Roman Empire, each with their own traditional customs, religious rites and gods. In New Testament times, sacrifice was the normal medium of prayer and worship, not merely for rural peasants and the then less civilized tribes of places like North Africa, Gaul and Britain, but also for the more sophisticated cultures of Greeks and Romans, Egyptians and Jews. For the most part, this would remain the case up to and beyond the conversion of the Emperor Constantine to Christianity. Sacrifice was one of those unarticulated cultural assumptions that never got explained, and we look in vain for a definition. Because they did not sacrifice to domestic, civic or imperial gods and goddesses, Christians were dubbed 'atheists', like Epicurean philosophers. It was normal, then, for prayers to be accompanied by gifts.

Clearly, people felt themselves to be part of a society which included supernatural beings who had an effect on their lives; and just as social transactions in most cultures are oiled by gifts, so commerce with these unseen powers had to be conducted in the same way. Thus there are countless examples of a city or individual in distress vowing to make rich offerings to some god if that divine person would render assistance immediately. It is not surprising that some scholars of previous generations spoke of such prayer as a *negotium* or business transaction.[8] But this hardly does justice to the wide range of motivations that can be discerned. If you want to celebrate something, you throw a party with lots of eats and drinks; if you want to express gratitude, you give a box of chocolates; and gifts and greetings cards are associated with birthdays and retirements, in other words with honouring people. When, years ago, my youngster broke a neighbour's window, reconciliation took the form of a visit, an apology, and not merely restitution in repairing the window but a bunch of flowers and a box of chocolates. It is such analogies which help us to appreciate the highly concrete expressions of prayer which sacrifice constituted.

In other words, many prayers may have been requests accompanied by the equivalent of bribery and corruption; but that kind of behaviour does not exhaust the notion of prayer. Thanksgiving, veneration, repentance, celebration, being in relationship or restoring relationships, dealing with guilt, impurity, or alienation, getting rid of hostile and evil influences, buying off divine anger, or enjoying peace, love, joy and hope — all of these things were involved in religious rites which expressed prayer to gods or daemons.[9] Prayer always involved a great deal more than the petition and intercession which is so vulnerable to the empiricist's critique.

Many, of course, conceived of the gods as like human beings writ large, needing the same things as human beings need, participating in the sacrificial feasts as their portion of meat was consumed in the fire. So, not to perform these rituals would displease the gods and bring about dire consequences. These views were subject to criticism and satire from a very early date, but clearly persisted. In the second century CE, the satirist Lucian pictured the gods in heaven looking down and waiting for sacrifices to be offered: if a sacrifice is being performed, all mouths are open to feast on the smoke; like flies they settle on the altar to drink up the trickling streams of blood.[10] So sacrifice was lampooned for treating the gods as inferior to human beings; from Aristotle on, it had been attacked by philosophers on these grounds, as had the notion that the gods were capricious and could be bribed. Socrates, it seems, had even earlier insisted that sacrifice made no difference: it was prayerful desire for virtue that alone was of value in the endeavour to keep the favour of the gods. His influence was felt by Plato and, subsequently, the popular moral philosophers so evident in the urban society of St Paul's Mediterranean world.[11]

So a theological critique emerged: it was unworthy of the dignity, sanctity and integrity of the gods to offer sacrifice. The divine must be conceived as above such influence – consistent, unchangeable, impassible – not, like human beings, given to favouritism or subject to emotional whim. From a moral standpoint, sacrifice with selfish mercenary motives was unacceptable. The only worthwhile prayer was for spiritual qualities, notably virtue. From this discussion, there emerged the ideal of the 'philosopher's prayer', which owed much to this long-standing critique of popular religion.[12] It is well represented by the meditations of Marcus Aurelius, the Stoic emperor of the second century CE:

> Live with the gods. For that person truly lives with them, who, all life long, lays bare the soul to heaven, showing that it is a soul well content with the dispositions of providence, and executing every wish of that divinity which Zeus has given to be a person's guardian and guide – a fragment of the divine self. And this divinity is the understanding and reason of each one of us.[13]

Thus prayer came to be conceived as communion between the divine and human, based on their kinship and likeness, and dependent on human virtue and endeavour to imitate the gods. Material sacrifice was rejected, and replaced by 'rational sacrifices', understood in terms of moral qualities, religious ecstasy and prayer, above all adoration and thanksgiving.

So it was that pagans and Christians expressed many of the same sentiments about prayer in the literature of the third to fifth centuries CE, though they differed in their practice. Neoplatonists increasingly defended traditional religious rites, while Christians attacked them, claiming greater consistency in rejecting sacrifice as unworthy and inappropriate. But sacrificial language was used of Christian prayer and sacraments, good works and martyrdom, and at the heart of Christian belief and worship was the death of Christ understood as a sacrifice. Both philosopher and Christian apologist needed to justify prayer morally and theologically, and both alike focused on the purified character of the worshipper in communion with the divine.

Petition and placation came to be regarded as inconsistent with God's benevolent changelessness, and the Neoplatonist Porphyry saw thanksgiving as the only proper motive for sacrifice to the gods.[14] To the Supreme God, he thought, no sacrifice could be offered, for even a word was too material; pure silence was the only worship appropriate, holy sacrifice being offered by close contact with the divine and by being transformed into the divine likeness, until the offering was perfected by achieving passionlessness of soul and contemplation of God. Iamblichus, another Neoplatonist, takes a sort of ecological view, the union and harmony of the universe being cemented by sublimating the life of the animal in sacrifice, which is not complete without prayer; together, prayer and sacrifice create an indissoluble bond of fellowship with the gods. Purification and imitation of the gods is the goal.[15]

Likewise, the Christian Origen, inheriting the prophetic attacks on sacrifice in the Greek version of the Hebrew Bible as well as the philosophical critique we have been tracing, had insisted that the Supreme God could only be worshipped by spiritual sacrifices. The spiritual altar was the mind of faithful Christians; spiritual images of God were the virtues implanted in human beings by God's Word; the Body of Christ was a spiritual temple; Christian people continually celebrated spiritual feasts and fasts by constant prayer and abstention from wickedness. The sacrifice of Christ was an example of obedience, love and self-offering. Loyalty and devotion to God is to be expressed in a good moral life, in charity, in thanksgiving and praise, and in communion with God. God does not need sacrifice, but prefers mercy and a humbled spirit, says Origen, echoing both the biblical and philosophic tradition.[16]

Like the philosophers, Origen was concerned that prayers and sacrifices be worthy of God. A God who is known spiritually should not be worshipped materially, but by piety and virtue. So separation from the material and earthly, imitation and contemplation of the passionless divine life, also began to affect the expression of Christian spirituality. God needs and desires nothing; indeed, God already possesses everything, so human beings can give God nothing. Since God cannot really be affected by prayer, prayer has more to do with the human need to be detached from sin and, through worship, become like God. But if God is just, and so cannot be bent by prayers and offerings, what would be the point of repentance, Origen enquires. Why pray if God's attitude cannot be changed? In his treatise *On Prayer* he appeals to free will; justifying prayer, within God's dispensation for the universe and the soul, as the revelation of a person's faith and ultimate desire.[17] Other Christian writers (from Clement of Alexandria to Gregory Nazianzen) echo the sentiment that the only worthy gift to God is one's self, purified from sin and giving honour to God. We can sum up this discussion with words of Porphyry, the pagan philosopher, quoted by the Christian Augustine:

> For God indeed, being the Father of all, is in need of nothing; but for us it is good to adore God by means of justice, charity and other virtues, and thus to make life itself a prayer to God, by inquiring into and imitating the divine nature. For inquiring purifies us, and imitation deifies us, by moving us nearer to God.[18]

Compared with this kind of sophisticated discussion, the empiricist's demand for proof of answer to prayer surely seems rather crude. It reduces prayer to the kind of bargaining with God that the ancients could see only too well to be theologically inappropriate, and fails to appreciate the much broader range and dynamics of prayer as practised by religious people – and I mean here and now, not just in the period I have been surveying. Even without the sophistications of the philosophers, the ancients knew that at the heart of prayer is thanksgiving and praise, purification and dedication, that prayer is as much about proper receiving as about asking. Indeed, prayer has been described as being attuned to glory and pain, the agony and ecstasy of the universe;[19] and in the Jewish and Christian tradition, prayer is in fact, above all, a corporate commemoration, the bringing to mind, or recollection, of a sacred history which draws the worshipper into a community and a narrative that both gives identity and puts the individual into perspective, eliciting a response of praise, thanksgiving, repentance, and obedience or renewal.

Theology and prayer

The other point to emerge from the ancient discussion we have surveyed is the intimate link between the practice of prayer and the concept of God. *Lex orandi lex credendi*, and vice versa, we might say: in other words, prayer informs belief, and belief informs prayer. The discourse of prayer is therefore central to any theological enquiry. In fact, some of the greatest contributions to Christian theology have in the past been in the form of prayer (the *Confessions* of St Augustine, for example), or at least in a genre, such as the homily or sermon, intended to play a role in a liturgical setting. But for now let us focus on parallels between the ancient discussion just surveyed and one of the central theological issues in the modern world.

It might appear that the question of God's existence is now the principal uncertainty; and, as we should have noticed, this barely entered the discussion in antiquity. But, actually, that presenting problem overlays another issue, the same issue as was at stake in the ancient world, and an issue which profoundly divides those who lay claim to some form of religious belief: namely the question how God relates to the world, and whether God intervenes. The empiricist, in demanding proof of answer to prayer, betrays the need for evidence of God's activity as an indicator of God's existence. Many believers look for signs of God's intervention, feeling their faith insecure without the proof of miracle or evident spiritual effect. But what kind of a God is presupposed by the demand that prayer be answered in the way apparently implied? What kind of a God provides empty parking-lots for self-important favourites, while letting innocent children starve in Africa and die in Bosnia? Believer and empiricist are in the same case, and both are open to the same kind of criticisms as prophets and philosophers offered 2,000 years ago. They have forgotten that, in traditional theology, the orderly progression of nature was the principal sign of God's creative activity and providential care; not the inconsistency and capriciousness implied by breaks in nature's laws.

I know a minister of religion who was deeply disturbed by what seemed an answer to prayer: he asked 'Why me?', not in the face of disaster, but in the face of blessing beyond hope or expectation. It is not just scientific explanation, but profound theological insight that suggests that a God of justice and integrity must be beyond arbitrary manipulation. That should remain good theological grounds for the view that God is changeless and consistent, impassible in the sense of not being affected or moved from impartiality by any pleas or bargains. It is not surprising that what emerged in the critique of religion in the ancient world was a concept of the divine expressed in negative terms, emphasizing the 'otherness' of God, as invisible, intangible, incorporeal, unchangeable, immortal, inexpressible, incomprehensible, infinite: for most concepts of God are mental idols. Believers who claim to have God in their pockets have diminished God. The great twentieth-century contemplative Thomas Merton was a bright modern student in the 1930s, one who dabbled in psychology and communism, one for whom faith in God was outmoded – until he came across the notion of God's aseity in medieval philosophy; that is, the idea that God's being is not conditioned or dependent upon anything else but the divine self.

> I had never had an adequate notion of what Christians meant by God. I had simply taken for granted that the God in whom religious people believed and to whom they attributed the creation and government of all things, was a noisy and dramatic and passionate character, a vague, jealous, hidden being, the objectification of all their own subjective ideals.[20]

One of the deep attractions of Eastern Orthodoxy is a liturgy that expresses that refusal to reduce God to a human projection. *Lex orandi lex credendi.*

Some of the same motivations lie behind those radical theologians who are now protesting at the 'reification' of God. Their position is the natural outcome of a theology which has ceased to be able to cope with miracle and intervention, from the eighteenth-century Deists to the present. The story is well known and I need not repeat it. As science explained everything, so God died the death of a thousand qualifications. An ineffective God is a non-existent God. Religion becomes a *blik* which has the beneficial effect of producing a certain way of life, but God makes no difference. The non-realist God of Don Cupitt and the Sea of Faith group has many attractions because it escapes the crunch issues as they seem to confront believers today. And they can continue to pray, as David Hart has shown in his recent book, *Faith in Doubt: Non-Realism and Christian Belief*:

> Prayer is experienced as freedom from the bondage imposed by the alienating forces and as a liberating experience making connections between the human world and the natural world of which humankind is one contributing part. In the religious vision, the barrier dividing Nature as subject and object is lifted in the imagination and a universal harmony is re-established.[21]

So the 'philosopher's prayer' lives again, but without an objectified God. Hart proceeds to give a non-realist account of the liturgies of the sacraments, treating them as 'signifiers' with a non-literal meaning, as genuinely 'outward and visible signs of an inward and spiritual grace', symbols of corporate commitment to one another, giving 'a right sense of ourselves in our human context', 'worshipping neither a being out there nor yet ourselves', but expressing 'the unity of self with the rest of the living world'. Intercession is 'an intensified concentration of the mind upon the other's well-being', or as Cupitt put it, 'gives formality, weight and seriousness of purpose to my care for Peter by binding it up with moral and religious values that are most precious to me'.[22]

Thus the subject of prayer becomes a kind of litmus test for particular theological proposals; and if I have appeared to be critical of the credulous, let me say that I do not regard the non-realist proposal as any more satisfactory. The emptying of the churches reflects the logical outcome of uncertainty about the reality of God. This is compounded, I believe, by the failure of many modern people to cope with the omnipresence, meaningfulness and truth of non-literal language – a subject which, if space permitted, might have occupied a fair proportion of this chapter, since the language of prayer and worship certainly needs deconstructing, and the substitution of mere silence is far from adequate. At least the non-realist position challenges our linguistic idols and reminds us that language itself is a sign and a symbol. But, be that as it may, I cannot but believe that the outcome of the non-realist position will be not just the death of God, but the death of theology, along with Christianity. Our concepts of God may inevitably be idols, and God may be inexpressible and unknowable, ultimately elusive, yet R. S. Thomas provokes us further:

I pray and incur
silence. Some take that silence
for refusal.
        I feel the power
that, invisible, catches me
by the sleeve, nudging
        towards the long shelf
that has the book on it, I will take down
        and read and find the antidote to an ailment.
        I know its ways with me;
how it enters my life,
        is present rather
before I perceive it, sunlight quivering
on a bare wall . . .

It has the universe
        to be abroad in.
There is nothing I can do
but fill myself with my own
        silence, hoping it will approach
        like a wild creature to drink
there, or perhaps like Narcissus
to linger a moment over its transparent face.[23]

There is a great deal more in that poem than at first meets the eye. Not for nothing was Thomas's silence given form by the traditions of Christian theology. The invisible 'Other', contrary to all expectation, takes the initiative. The wild creature comes unpredictably, like the wind that blows where it listeth, and the divine image is reflected in the face of the contemplative. As Thomas Merton put it,

> There is no true spiritual life outside the love of Christ. We have a spiritual life only because we are loved by Him. The spiritual life consists in receiving the gift of the Holy Spirit – the same Spirit which proceeds from the Word and from the Father, and who is Jesus' love for the Father.[24]

From the aseity of God, which was so important for Merton and excludes the possibility of what we might call human 'success' in prayer, there emerges a dynamic of divine love which reaches out through Christ and through the Holy Spirit, enabling the possibility of the human creature being so caught up in the mutual life of the Trinity that prayer becomes participation in that loving. Within that context, even 'asking' may release new possibilities. In John 15.7, the ones who can ask whatever they like and receive it are the ones who dwell in Christ, and whose asking is informed by that indwelling.

It is not often realized that crucial elements in the formation of the characteristic Christian concept of God as Trinity were the recognition of God's 'Otherness' and the need to give a satisfactory account of prayer. That Christ and the Holy Spirit must share fully in the divine nature was persuasive in the end because otherwise human nature had not been re-formed according to the divine image, nor were human creatures sanctified by the divine Spirit in the sacraments.[25] In the face of contemporary logicians who wanted to define God, so reducing the divine Being to comprehensibility on the pretext of not compromising divine transcendence, the great Cappadocian Fathers insisted on God's infinity and indefinability, on the Trinitarian Being of the divine,[26] a notion which breaks apart the categories of human thinking, while enabling participation through prayer and worship in the divine life of love.

For Gregory of Nyssa, knowledge of God meant entering the darkness of the Cloud of Presence, having nothing to hold on to or grasp, experiencing vertigo.[27] He represents that Greek Christian tradition in which prayer was, indeed, the test of the true theologian. For it was only the theologian who submitted to the discipline of mental and moral stripping who could in any way know God: the true theologian must qualify by purification and humility, they thought, for knowledge of God was the fruit of strict moral and intellectual asceticism. The best theologian, according to Gregory of

Nazianzus, is not the one who can give a complete logical account of the subject, but the one who 'assembles more of Truth's image and shadow'.[28]

Or, as Cardinal Newman put it, 'The mind is below truth not above it, and is bound not to descant upon it, but to venerate it'.[29] Perhaps the claim to autonomy has presented an even greater obstacle to the practice of prayer in the modern world than the empiricist demand. Many dare not admit contingency, vulnerability, creatureliness, imperfection and mortality. Nor are most people comfortable venerating anyone or anything. To return to Merton:

> The surest sign that we have received a spiritual understanding of God's love for us is the appreciation of our own poverty in the light of His infinite mercy.[30]

Prayer, then, has always been the test case for the analysis and assessment of particular theological positions. A genuinely open theological enquiry, which recognizes the necessity of exploring both outside and inside perspectives, cannot ignore the discourse of prayer.

Public and private

So far, however, much of what we have said could be confined to the sphere of personal prayer, the private activities of the individual worshipper or theologian. Our concern in this book is to address the issue of theological language in public. What I want to explore now is the interface between the private and the public, an area where we noted earlier a certain disjunction in our society.

What might appear to be the private spirituality of Thomas Merton, or, indeed, the Cappadocians, was in fact rooted in the public tradition of the Church's liturgy.

> Nourished by the Sacraments and formed by the prayer and teaching of the Church, we need seek nothing but the particular place willed for us by God within the Church . . . Then we discover what the spiritual life really is . . . It is not a matter of any special psychological effect in our own soul. It is the silence of our whole being in compunction and adoration before God, in the habitual realization that He is everything and we are nothing . . . That our life and strength proceed from Him . . . that it is absurd to live as though without Him . . . that, in the end, the only thing that matters is His glory.[31]

As noted earlier, in both Jewish and Christian tradition prayer has involved corporate commemoration or recollection of a sacred history which draws the worshipper into a narrative that both gives identity and creates community. The interface of the public and private comes in the recitation of psalms or the singing of hymns, where each and every one is 'I' and all are 'I' together:

I will exalt you O God my king:
I will bless your name for ever and ever.
One generation shall praise your works to another;
and declare your mighty acts.
Men shall recount the power of your terrible deeds;
and I will proclaim your greatness.[32]

My general point is this: the interface of the public and private is formative for both.

But the public nature of Jewish and Christian worship goes beyond the formation of like-minded communities. In fact, all the great religious traditions have embraced an important dialectic between the 'communalism' encouraged by belonging to and identifying with a particular group and its history, and a universal perspective.[33] One of the most intriguing features of second-century Christianity is its refusal, despite being a marginalized, persecuted group, to take the way of private spirituality. This can be seen in the struggle with the so-called Gnostics, and in the defence of traditions of public responsibility received from the Jewish community which was the matrix from which Christian groups sprang.

Jews had certain privileges under Roman law, one being exemption from the demand to share in imperial and civic rites of a religious kind (it's tempting to say 'on grounds of conscience', but that would be to introduce a very modern way of looking at it: it was actually based on respect for ancestral customs). In return, Jews would pray for the emperor in their synagogues as part of their prayers for the whole universe of which God was King. This sense of public responsibility, this public dimension to prayer, was something Christians adopted (see, for example, 1 Tim 2.1ff.). Conversely, by the time of the Cappadocians in the fourth century, the obvious public role of a church patronized by the government was counterbalanced by the reservation of the sacraments as more private mysteries for the initiated. The church community constituted an important interface between public and private, and prayer in each domain shaped the other.

To explore this interface further, I want to take you on another journey into foreign territory – not this time the past, though I suspect this trip will give us a kind of indirect access to the world of the past we were exploring earlier. The anthropologist Susan Starr Sered has published a study of the religious lives of elderly Jewish women in Jerusalem, more particularly the lives of Oriental Jewish women, women from Kurdistan, Turkey, the Yemen and elsewhere, who had made *aliya* to the land of Israel in their youth, and had grown old, most of them widowed, in the land of promise.[34] They came from a traditional, sexually segregated society. Significantly, the title of the book is *Women as Ritual Experts*.

These were women confined to the sphere of the domestic and the family; the private world, if you like. Synagogue was men's business. The women were illiterate and excluded from the public life of Jewish religion, explicitly centred as it is on the Sacred Book and the study of Torah. The study is particularly fascinating in highlighting the demarcation of separate territory and divergent concerns which allowed women to develop their own religious space, with its own rituals and symbolic language — for not only were they illiterate, they were linguistically impoverished, unable to articulate concepts except by broken sentences completed through gesture.

To go into much detail would take too long, but there are key elements which I would like to try and list:

(1) The women, particularly now they were old and less pressed by the necessities of child-rearing, were preoccupied with the health and welfare of their families, both ancestors and descendants, and saw in this a religious duty. Their role was to ensure that blessings were obtained for all those for whom they had responsibility. Such blessings were sought from pilgrimages to the tombs of the saints, the lighting of candles, the kissing of *mezuzot*, helping neighbours and the giving of alms, especially to the rabbi for the religious school.

(2) The religious competence of the women especially centred around the preparation of food, the sacralizing of the everyday. Their relationship to religious festivals was particularly shaped by their own domestic roles, the need to purify the domestic world for Passover, and to prepare the special foods appropriate to each occasion. In this respect, men were dependent upon their good offices.

(3) Although regarding themselves as good Jews who kept the commandments, in fact the women developed their own religious traditions, and sat fairly loose to the rabbi's notion of *halakah*. Whereas synagogue had figured little in their earlier child-bound lives, it now became important. The service was unintelligible to them, but the Sacred Scroll, which they could never read, became the focus of their prayers as they watched from the distance of the women's gallery. Their domestic family concerns were brought into the public religious world.

I guess for most traditional societies the roles of men and women have been clearly differentiated, and they have roughly followed the line between the private and public sphere. Certainly, in Christian, Jewish and Islamic societies, public religion has generally been male-dominated, theology has been concerned with truth-claims about the world as a whole, and liturgy has projected social norms onto the heavens, God being worshipped as a largely benevolent and fatherly, but also strict, Emperor, with his subservient court paying homage. Yet, alongside this, there has been the private world of personal piety, often acted out by women, without sophisticated verbal or conceptual articulation. So, as religion has got privatized and the public world secularized, men have increasingly permitted their wives to go to church, but rarely accompanied them. In many quarters, religion is seen as women's sphere. In Russia, the grandmothers kept the faith alive, and as you look round church congregations in the secularized West, you may well note the same phenomenon.

One serious issue is whether the ordination of women will reinforce this perception – that prayer, whether corporate or individual, is women's work, and largely reduced to a kind of superstitious domestic insurance. That is at least as worrying as women's rejection of Christianity because of its predominantly male symbolism. In a post-Christian world, where atheism is, in practice, the privileged position, the lack of a public religious discourse is not unlikely to consign religion to a private female ghetto, dismissed as irrelevant by men who think they know better. The interface between private and public in corporate liturgy will either be undermined, or it will be the creative growth point.

It could be becoming the latter, as a real partnership between men and women is forged, which on the one hand encourages women to move beyond the domestic scene to engage with the big, public questions of truth and social responsibility, and on the other hand brings particular, personal concerns into the community of public prayer. For, at least in the Christian tradition, one thing that is being affirmed in public worship is that God, though transcendent and incomprehensible, chose, as it were, to get the divine hands dirty, and get involved in the messy business of human everyday life. Intercession books in churches show that, because the world has become a global village, the domestic horizons of women's prayer have expanded, just as those elderly Jewish women had begun to include the lads of the Israeli army in the extended family for which they sought blessing. Praying communities have public concerns, even if the public world ignores praying communities. And if churches, and, indeed, other religious communities, are marginalized, it could just be that power lies in the margins. The traditions of monastic life have quietly persisted in most major religious traditions, 'liminal' groups, living on the margins of society, following a vocation of intercessory prayer, private communities with public concerns. Biblical tradition speaks of God's people as just such a priestly presence among the nations.

In many quarters, liturgy and prayer have already taken the global village seriously, and narrow horizons are then inevitably challenged. The implications of that global prayer have to be faced theologically. God is 'out there' in the public, pluralist world, before self-important evangelists, tentative intercessors or religious dialogue people of whatever complexion emerge from their dens. To be true to their own tradition, Christians must surely affirm particulars, in all their diversity, without losing sight of the whole of creation. Maybe the public celebration of a diversity which both affirms and relativizes the identity of each is not beyond our imagining. For whatever we make of God, to be God at all, God must be God of the universe, not a private charm hidden around my neck, or yours. That public truth is again captured in the privacy of R. S. Thomas's solitariness. With his words I end:

Moments of great calm,
Kneeling before an altar
Of wood in a stone church
In summer, waiting for the God
To speak; the air a staircase
For silence . . .
  Prompt me, God;
But not yet. When I speak,
Though it be you who speak
Through me, something is lost.
The meaning is in the waiting.[35]

Notes

1. R. S. Thomas, 'Via Negativa' in *H'm* (London: Macmillan, 1972–75), p. 16.
2. Revd Dr J. Gordon Davies, Edward Cadbury Professor 1960–86.
3. Hugh McLeod, Chapter 1 above.
4. Ecclesiastes 3.7.
5. L. P. Hartley, *The Go-Between*, Prologue: 'The past is a foreign country: they do things differently there' (*Oxford Dictionary of Quotations*, 242:34).
6. E.g. Cicero, *De Natura Deorum: On the Nature of the Gods*, trans. Horace C. P. McGregor (Penguin Classics, 1972).
7. Frances M. Young, *The Use of Sacrificial Ideas in Greek Christian Writers from the New Testament to John Chrysostom*, Cambridge University PhD thesis (Patristic Monograph Series, no. 5; Cambridge, MA: The Philadelphia Patristic Foundation, 1979). Popular version: *Sacrifice and the Death of Christ* (SPCK, 1975; SCM Press, 1983).
8. H. Schmidt, *Veteres philosophi quomodo iudicaverint de precibus* (Giessen, 1908), p. 1. Cf.

Guy Soury, *Aperçus de philosophe religieuse chez Maxime de Tyre* (Paris, 1942), ch. 2: 'La prière antique, ou le sacrifice qui en est un forme, n'est qu'un marché entre l'homme et la divinité, le premier cherchant à s'assurer une faveur ou en remerciant après l'avoir obtenue.'
9. *Daemones* (pl.) was a common word referring to supernatural beings or spirits, some benign, others malevolent, usually not the 'high gods', but lesser divine beings. Subsequent Christian perspectives which identified the benign with angels and the malevolent with devils led to the English derivation 'demons'.
10. Lucian, *Peri thuseōn*, 1 and 9.
11. This is a summary account, for which full references should be sought in the works cited in note 7 above.
12. For detailed references concerning the development of the philosopher's prayer, see works cited in note 7 above.
13. *The Thoughts of Marcus Aurelius*, trans. John Jackson (The World's Classics; OUP, 1906), p. 42, slightly altered in the interests of inclusive language!
14. Porphyry (*c.* 232–303 CE) was the successor of Plotinus, in fact Plotinus' editor. Both Plotinus (*c.* 205–270 CE) and the Christian scholar Origen (*c.* 185–254 CE) are reputed to have been pupils of Ammonius Saccas, often regarded as the founder of Neoplatonism. Iamblichus (*c.* 250–330 CE) is the third great philosopher of the Neoplatonist school. Porphyry wrote a notorious work against the Christians.
15. For detailed references and discussion, see works cited in note 7 above; and also Frances M. Young, 'The idea of sacrifice in Neoplatonic and Patristic texts', *Studia Patristica* ix (1972), pp. 278–81.
16. Origen's awareness of the philosophic discussion is evident from the fact that many of these points are made in his apologetic work *Contra Celsum*, but they are also written into his biblical exegesis. For detailed references, see my discussions elsewhere, cited in note 7 above.
17. Origen, *On Prayer*, 5.1 – 10.2.
18. Augustine, *The City of God*, xix.23.
19. E.g. (by implication if not in so many words) Ann and Barry Ulanov, 'Prayer and personality: prayer as primary speech' in Cheslyn Jones, Geoffrey Wainwright and Edward Yarnold SJ (eds), *The Study of Spirituality* (London: SPCK, 1986), pp. 24–33.
20. Thomas Merton, *Elected Silence* (English edition of *The Seven Storey Mountain*; Hollis and Carter, 1949), pp. 139–40.
21. David A. Hart, *Faith in Doubt: Non-Realism and Christian Belief* (London: Mowbray, 1993), p. 79.
22. Cupitt as quoted in Hart, ibid., p. 82.
23. R. S. Thomas, 'The presence' in *Between Here and Now* (London: Macmillan, 1981), p. 107.
24. Thomas Merton, *Thoughts in Solitude* (London: Burns and Oates, 1958 (1975, 1993)), p. 37.
25. This is clearly implied by both Athanasius, *De Incarnatione* and Basil, *De Spiritu Sancto*. See further my articles 'God and religious language' in W. R. Schoedel and Robert Wilken, *Early Christian Literature and the Greek Intellectual Tradition*, Festschrift for R. M. Grant (Théologie Historique 53; Paris: Editions Beauchesne, 1979); and 'God: an essay in patristic theology', *The Modern Churchman* 29 (1981), pp. 149–65.
26. The works of both Basil of Caesarea and Gregory of Nyssa *Against Eunomius*, and the *Theological Orations* of Gregory of Nazianzus, demonstrate this point.
27. See the introduction by Jean Daniélou to *From Glory to Glory*, a collection of extracts from Gregory of Nyssa's mystical writings, trans. H. Musurillo (New York: Charles Scribner's Sons, 1961); also now *Gregory of Nyssa, The Life of Moses*, trans., introd. and notes by Abraham J. Malherbe and Everett Ferguson, preface by John Meyendorff

(Classics of Western Spirituality; New York: Paulist Press, 1978).
28. See the first of Gregory of Nazianzus' *Theological Orations*. The translation by Lionel Wickam and Frederick Williams and commentary by F. W. Norris in *Faith Gives Fullness to Reasoning: The Five Theological Orations of Gregory of Nazianzus* (Leiden: Brill, 1991) is particularly helpful.
29. John H. Newman, *Essay on the Development of Christian Doctrine*, ed. J. M. Cameron (Penguin Classics, 1974), p. 256; quoted in a similar connection in my inaugural lecture, 'The critic and the visionary', published by the University of Birmingham (1987), and in *Scottish Journal of Theology* 41 (1988), pp. 297–312.
30. Merton, *Thoughts in Solitude*, op. cit., pp. 37–8.
31. Ibid., p. 52.
32. Psalm 145.1, 4, 6; version *Methodist Hymn Book* 884.
33. Cf. the contribution to this book by John Hull, Chapter 2 above.
34. Susan Starr Sered, *Women as Ritual Experts: The Religious Lives of Elderly Jewish Women in Jerusalem* (New York and Oxford: OUP, 1992).
35. R. S. Thomas, 'Kneeling' in *Selected Poems 1946–1968* (London: Granada Publishing, 1979; reissue of 1973 collection), p. 119.

11
Constructing a public theology

David F. Ford

I like Theodore![1] His liberated and liberating desire to see the face of God is a good image for the coming together of interiority and exteriority that runs through much of this book. Theodore shows that Werner Ustorf has inherited something of the spirit of his predecessor as Professor of Mission in Birmingham, Walter Hollenweger, embodying both the role of the imagination and the importance of the marginalized in doing theology. At the same time, he raises a question that is profoundly disturbing for Western theology and its secular antagonists and discussion partners: 'whether the Western project of dominance and oppression since 1492 was related to the domestication of the Western soul, and the colonization of the quest for God within' (above, p. 101). There is a comparably radical question (this time directed towards 'the enterprise of theology') in Isabel Wollaston's abrupt ending. Her apparent doubt about whether theology can sustain an open question that amounts to a fundamental conflict is expressed in a delicate 'perhaps it is significant', immediately overpowered by the final word that, as regards theology, 'Wiesel is vehemently opposed to any such enterprise' (above, p. 86).

The history of Western colonialism and imperialism might be seen as the most obvious world-wide manifestation of a pathology which reached its point of greatest intensity in Europe in the Holocaust, and whose ecological implications are discussed by Rex Ambler. The philosopher Edith Wyschogrod, in her gripping analysis of our century as one of 'man-made mass death',[2] has seen such events not only as closely connected with the nature of modernity, but also as pervasively significant for the way in which we should think about the world. It is of Copernican dimensions: not to take this 'death event' of our century seriously is to do the equivalent of flat-earth or geocentric thinking.

This puts the concern with Western public theology in a perspective that simultaneously raises questions about the modern university (pioneered in Berlin), about the churches and other religious communities, and about late capitalist society. It is now clearer, since the fall of many Communist regimes and the breakup of the Soviet Union, that the religions of the world are crucial to its future in ways that few discerned earlier this century. There are few trouble spots without a strong religious element; and that is just the visible, negative aspect of the direct significance of religious communities for probably between three and four billion of the world's population. The religions are deeply involved in the transformations at present happening around the world. Their leaders and ordinary members, as well as those who deal with them in political, economic, educational, cultural and legal matters, are having to give urgent and often ill-informed attention to issues of meaning, truth and practice that arise in relation to these communities. For all the reality of the easily caricatured 'fundamentalists' and 'fanatics', there are also present through all communities millions of intelligent believers, non-believers and agnostics, who desire to pay high quality attention to these issues.

For such people, universities are one obvious resource, but on the whole, as Stephen Pattison's devastating account (which I find somewhat hyperbolic) argues, they are not well served. The task is immense. It involves complex responsibilities exercised in relation to huge, interconnected global communities. There is the world-wide academic community in its various disciplines, few of which are irrelevant to theology – just in these Cadbury Lectures from one Department, the range of fields represented is impressive: history, sociology, education, health studies, psychology, psychoanalysis, literary criticism, Hebrew, Greek, ecology, philosophy, Holocaust studies, missiology, systematic theology and patristics. There are the major (and minor) religions and their global ramifications. And there is the global society of nations, in which the religions have a wide variety of public voices. If theology (and religious studies – I intend both when I talk of theology, in line with the meaning it has in the title of the Department which sponsored these lectures) is to do with responsibly thinking through questions of meaning, truth and practice in such contexts, then it seems to me to be hard to deny it a vital role in our academic, religious and national cultures. Yet, of course, it is not so simple, and some of the complexities and dilemmas are acutely revealed in this book.

My own dilemma is how to respond to the preceding chapters. The obvious option would be to write a review of them. But why pre-empt the next stage of their reception? What is appropriate to the present stage, when the lectures have been delivered, their texts have been gathered and the publisher is urgently requiring them? Reading through them it is apparent that, for obvious reasons, none of the writers has been able to engage with all of the other chapters. The job that seems waiting to be done is what I might call 'constructive appropriation'. It is, I suppose, what all of us try to do with a good book: certainly, to ask questions and criticize it, but above all to try to assimilate it, relating it to our own thinking. The preceding chapters themselves show a variety of ways of carrying on the discipline of theology today. During 15 years in the University of Birmingham Department of Theology, I found it a most suitable place to attempt to relate to the 'three publics' of academy, religious communities and society. So I will try now to draw on the rich resources of the preceding chapters in order to sketch some of the elements of a public theology that dares to speak of God.

I was struck by the number of fruitful concepts in the preceding chapters, and I will first of all go through them with a view to distilling what I find most appropriate to my project. I recognize that my synthesis may not be one that any of the authors would actually subscribe to: most of these concepts are very flexible in their use, and often my application is in tension with the original context. From time to time I will indicate how I differ from the author, but overall the emphasis is on a particular constructive appropriation. It is meant partly as a provocation to others to do something similar for themselves, and even to encourage the members of the Department in Birmingham to engage more thoroughly with each other's positions, if only in reaction against my 'misappropriation'. I also recognize that I am being highly selective and ignoring a good deal of each contribution.

The analogy of a language

Hugh McLeod's account of religious change in modern Britain mostly confirms what an educated common sense would guess, but two aspects stand out. The first is the description of 1880–1914 as a period during which a higher proportion of English children learnt Christian doctrine and ethics than at any other time before or since. The second is the description of the contemporary babel: increasing pluralism, the supersession of religious language by a variety of scientific and professional languages, and the secularization of political rhetoric. The vivid image is of a common language, a lingua franca, losing its primacy but finding no satisfactory successor. There are some specialist languages of particular groups, there is a sort of Esperanto which is too impoverished to fulfil the roles of the old lingua franca, and 'in some areas of life the result is simply a void. In others, the lack of any convincing alternatives means that most people cling to the old words' (above, p. 19).

The constructive questions which these points pose are whether it is possible to have the learning of Christian faith taken as seriously as the learning of a language in a multilingual community, and whether 'fluent Christian speakers' are able to develop their language in order to cope with unprecedented demands for translations, paraphrases and imaginative borrowings, while maintaining the basic grammar and syntax. Can Christianity continue to do in this culture what it has done and is doing in so many others, expressing its testimony in new forms and contexts, so as to enable an appropriation by and a transformation of the host culture? I am not speculating about whether this will be possible in the sense of becoming the 'majority religion', but whether there are resources in contemporary Christianity comparable to those which Frances Young describes in the transformative education (*paideia*) of the church in its early centuries, one of the marks of which was a sophisticated intellectual engagement with the best thought of Hellenistic civilization.[3] Similar questions can be raised about the other religions in our society, and, indeed about the other sets of linguistic and cultural practices which are in many ways functional equivalents to religions.

John Hull helps to focus some of these questions through the controversial area of worship in state schools. His fascinating analysis raises many of the key issues facing a public theology, and he also offers his own suggestions, which are likewise inevitably controversial. The state school is a good testing ground for ideas about public theology. Education is vital for any religion and any society that wants to continue, the formation of our children arouses the deepest passions, and in a pluralist society the tensions between the desire to have some common bonds and the affirmation of particular religious, cultural and other identities are bound to be intense. One constructive conclusion from this situation is that, because a society like ours must have public debates about these matters, the need for high quality public theology is all the more urgent, and it would be a dereliction of public responsibility for universities not to contribute to it. That should (!) act as a supporting argument for state support for universities that take this task seriously, but does not get us far as regards the character of public theology. John Hull poses the dilemmas brilliantly, and he devastatingly exposes the inadequacy of the Government's present policy. His close attention to legislation and explanatory directives from the Department of Education is itself an example of the sort of achievement that Stephen Pattison is claiming for theology. But what are John Hull's own proposals? The last three paragraphs of his chapter introduce ideas which are profoundly important for the conception of public theology, and are also, in various ways, taken up in other chapters.

First there is his use of the analogy of language in a rather different manner from Hugh McLeod. McLeod's use is in line with the sort of questions I generated from it above, seeing a particular religion as a way of construing and relating to the whole of reality in accordance with its own vocabulary, syntax, classic texts and so on. On this analogy you need, above all, to be fluent in one 'language' (or immersed in the ways of one 'culture'); and the greatest adequacy and creativity will come from a Shakespeare who has thoroughly mastered one tongue, rather than from someone who has a smattering of several. Of course, the linguistic ideal is to be fluent in more than one, and here the analogy with a religious community tends to break down. For a religion is about life commitments, participation in community, and the shaping of understanding and behaviour in pervasive ways which do not allow (at least in the self-understanding of the major religious communities) for simultaneous participation in more than one. It would be like living two lives. There are, of course, difficult or borderline cases, and new religions may develop from syncretisms, but then they are like a new language and simply add one more religion to the pluralist mix.

The difference in John Hull's use of the analogy is important. He accuses the Government of

> preventing any speech about God which might imply that God is not confined within a specific religious tradition . . . It is as if God were confined to the cultural, spiritual and religious traditions of human beings such that God could only be addressed in Hebrew or Arabic or Punjabi . . . My own view is that in religious education there can and should be speech about God both within each separate religious tradition and as being a reality beyond the limits of any one religious tradition or of all of them put together. God is great. God is that greater than which nothing can be conceived. (above, pp. 33–4)

He then quotes 1 Kings 8.27. So he quotes a particular tradition in order to claim that there can be speech about God beyond the limits of any tradition. He has accepted a quasi-spatial view of a 'language', rather than seeing it as a way of handling all reality (including relating to other traditions). While he allows that there can be speech about God 'within' each tradition, he also claims a 'view' transcending all of them, one which can see their 'limits'. Of course, any respectable concept of God does not claim to 'contain' God and does see God as relating to all reality – but it does this, as in 1 Kings, by having appropriated God through some tradition. What is John Hull's viewpoint? What is the source of his speaking about God beyond all traditions? It could be his own Christian tradition, or a development of it – in which case it is not a view beyond all traditions. But there is a more sinister possibility. Is there here a hint of a modern myth which bedevils so much public discussion of religious questions? This myth is that it is possible somehow to 'stand outside' or 'have an overview' of the religions. All the traditions are effectively patronized from a viewpoint which fails to make explicit its own commitments. The 'language' that is often, in fact, taught through religious education which is informed by this myth is one which has every claim to be considered seriously as a world-view that is held by many people. But it is necessary for it to be identified as just that (carrying with it a range of beliefs, practices, judgements and communal allegiances), rather than as a 'metalanguage' enabling a privileged overview. The public discussion of theological issues will take a great step forward when it is recognized that an ideology of neutrality (or, in Hugh McLeod's term, an Esperanto), claiming to be detached from or to transcend all traditions, can easily serve a strategy of domination. Recent critiques of various disciplines have pointed to these dangers in academic discourse. In religious education, I suspect that a great deal of often inarticulate dissatisfaction is created by the sense that what is being taught is not any genuine living 'language' at all: it is either a smattering of several, not even allowing students to be intelligent tourists; or it is an Esperanto of neutrality, enabling the study of these curious phenomena but actually hindering fluency in any one.

That is extreme, and it is a very contentious interpretation of John Hull (if not of common attitudes). My suspicions are aroused by his conclusion that his position 'demands a low theological definition'. That *could* mean that any rich and full understanding of God, as held by particular traditions, has to be set aside in favour of a God worshipped in Esperanto.

Reciprocal witness

But there is another reading of John Hull's conclusion which pivots around a fruitful concept that appears in various chapters. He advocates the 'spirit of reciprocal witness'. Emmanuel Lartey insists on 'taking seriously people's reports and stories of religious experience'. Werner Ustorf builds his whole lecture around such reports. Isabel Wollaston likewise makes testimony her main category. Gareth Jones 'understands truth as itself established in witness and in testimony' (above, p. 115); and Frances Young sees Jewish and Christian prayer as

> above all, a corporate commemoration, the bringing to mind, or recollection, of a sacred history which draws the worshipper into a community and a narrative that both gives identity and puts the individual into perspective, eliciting a response of praise, thanksgiving, repentance, and obedience or renewal. (above, p. 139)

What would happen if John Hull's understanding of witness were to turn out to be more like those of Gareth Jones and Frances Young? There would then be no suspicion of anyone claiming a viewpoint beyond all traditions. Reciprocal witness could be the key idea for a public theology.

How might that work out? The voluminous treatment of themes such as witness, testimony, memory, proclamation, attestation, confession and martyrdom in recent Christian theology suggests a very long answer just from that family of traditions. The term itself is obviously flexible and can be given very varied content. But at the heart of its value in formal terms are three features.

Firstly, it insists on the priority of self-description in any approach to a faith or world-view. Each must be approached through its own testimony, and we ourselves are encouraged to articulate the full meaning of our own faith for others. And if our testimony includes witnessing to brokenness, despair, or other great suffering, then the 'self' (corporate and personal) that is attested may well have that character of fragmentation so well evoked by Gareth Jones. All sorts of other discourses, critical and constructive, can join in too, but priority is given to testimony.

Secondly, the reciprocity of the witness sets up a dynamic of pluralist communication whose results are unpredictable. Who can tell what will happen as diverse testimonies are communicated, interpreted and lived with? There can be bitter clashes, irresolvable disputes, withdrawals from contact, or reinforcement of alienation; there can also be fresh insight into one's own and others' faiths, openings for undreamt of developments and enrichments, or a conviction of what John Hull calls a 'single spiritual vocation of humanity' (above, p. 33). Witness can be a dangerous thing, focusing the deepest passions, the most zealous energies and the clearest illuminations. But putting such an activity at the centre of public theology is simply being honest about the ambivalent power of religion in our world. To have anything less vigorous or more domesticated would be to fail to do justice to the nature of religions. It should never be forgotten that when the public square has been officially cleared of religion the result has never been a vacuum — our century has been full of alternatives whose record has at least equalled the worst that the religions have sponsored. Werner Ustorf's question about the colonization of the quest for God in the West is worth further discussion.

Thirdly, reciprocal witness gives a pointer towards a reconception of boundaries, another theme which recurs throughout the book. Instead of spatial metaphors, which tend to encourage seeing boundaries as separating, or dividing and only touching along the border, we might see boundaries constituted by the quality of communication between people and groups. Good communication enables boundaries to be internalized in each party, so that we carry the 'others' in our hearts and minds, constantly allowing them to inform and question us. This mutual indwelling is extraordinarily demanding – or, theologically speaking, an amazing grace. Its limit case is when there is not only no mutuality, but testimony is received with rejection and hostility. Simon Kimbangu's martyrdom is a paradigm of fruitful witness which needs to be borne constantly in mind in a century during which perhaps more members of various religions have been killed for their public testimony to God (or simply their identification with a religious community) than in any other (above, p. 110).

Construction

So, taking the language analogy in Hugh McLeod's sense and a concept of witness as developed above, what further resources for a constructive public theology might be gathered from the preceding chapters?

Stephen Pattison can contribute a vivid portrayal of the public theologian. He pictures an 'artist and critic of belief, myth, metaphor and symbol'; a 'practitioner of transformational and reflective knowledge', traditionally called wisdom; and a 'purveyor of distinctively theologically-derived methods, concepts and insights' (above, pp. 41ff.). The imperative of witness is implied in the dual conviction that runs through the chapter: that there are resources of wisdom in the religions, and that they must be communicated comprehensibly in relation to other disciplines and spheres of society.

Emmanuel Lartey testifies to a self that can be both theologian and therapist, to their mutual enrichment. The conception of personhood as formed interactively, especially through internalizing interpersonal experiences, is shown to be well suited to being brought into synthesis with a multifaceted and nuanced kind of 'God-talk'. Why is it so hard for many 'moderns' to imagine how millions of people at least as intelligent, well-educated and psychologically sophisticated as themselves can actually believe in God with integrity? It is the sort of imaginative problem that any dominant ideology which has attained the status of 'common sense' tends to have (and Christianity had a comparable problem for centuries in Europe). Emmanuel Lartey allows us to 'imagine otherwise' by offering a chapter that embodies an integration of therapy and theology. A recent philosophical version of a concept of self hospitable to theology, which also makes explicitly central the activity of 'attestation', is that of Paul Ricoeur in *Oneself as Another*.[4] Ricoeur is even more radical about the otherness that is intrinsic to the notion of self, and that, it seems to me, is a very fruitful line of thought for a public theology with the activity of respectful witness at its heart.

Paul Joyce describes the transition of the Bible from being an accepted public point of authoritative reference to being a public book in relation to a whole range of disciplines united by a hermeneutical concern. Even beyond church and academy it plays diverse roles as a cultural classic. To be alert contemporary readers of this book is to find ourselves needing to relate to all three of the publics for theology.

Rex Ambler's question, 'Where on earth is God?', is answered by critically adopting aspects of 'beyond', 'here' and 'ahead'. The question perceptively identifies a fundamental change in the nature of 'late modern' concern about God. No longer are the main questions the traditional ones of the philosophy of religion: 'Does God exist?' and 'What is God's nature?' Now the question is about the location of God, if any. Bonhoeffer is one of the most perceptive of the theological wrestlers with this question. Rex Ambler quotes Bonhoeffer on God being 'edged out of the world'. He does not complete the quotation: '. . . onto the cross'. Bonhoeffer's way of developing a public theology is very different from Rex Ambler's. The former works through the resources of a particular 'language' (Christianity understood in terms of incarnation, death and resurrection, critically discussed and developed in some fresh ways); the latter, in its use of general concepts floating free of identifiable contemporary communities of belief, worship and mutual commitment, feels to me more like an Esperanto. That has its uses, but I suspect that it cannot grip deeply enough or resonate richly enough to answer the question of God's whereabouts adequately. I would go Bonhoeffer's way, or (with more reservations) that of his current interpreter Eberhard Jüngel, who likewise makes central the question about where God is.[5] But I recognize that it is an approach which, in the public realm, has its handicaps which Esperantist alternatives are deliberately designed to overcome. It is part of the strength of the University of Birmingham Department of Theology that it has for many years been able to offer students and a wider public examples of both approaches in operation.

But even within Rex Ambler's own framework I would suggest exploring, in terms of an analogy of location which has something more to offer than 'beyond', 'here' and 'ahead', the possibilities of Werner Ustorf's suggestion of 'before the face of God'. This, significantly, primarily locates us in relation to God rather than vice versa, and it implies the priority of God. In both the Bible and Werner Ustorf it also allows for absence in complex ways (the hiding of the face, the turning away of the face, the cry of dereliction, the non-experience of God and many other expressions). In addition, it gives a theological description of the public realm which overcomes any dichotomy of public and private – both are most fundamentally described as being 'before God'.

Gareth Jones and Frances Young offer complementary examples of public theology which are a most fitting culmination of the book. My construction would include them as epitomes of what is meant by a systematic theology and an intellectual spirituality which are involved with the three publics of academy, religious communities and the rest of society, and, through that complex engagement, are led into fresh articulations of classic themes.

But what of 'Religious language after the Holocaust'? Claude Lanzmann's *Shoah* has been the most important film I have seen: nine hours in a London cinema immersed in testimony to the details of the Holocaust. Isabel Wollaston's quotation from Raul Hilberg on the priority of description, of gathering the minutiae of these events to give a fuller picture, does go to the heart of Lanzmann's approach.[6] She shows how, even for those who suffered it, speaking of God has been possible for some, but not for others. It is 'an open question, a conflict' (above, p. 86); and no one can claim an overview of it. As she suggests, there is theology with which this lack of overview is incompatible. Is there also theology which can do justice to radical contradiction among witnesses, fragmentation, the inadequacy of all theodicy, the requirement of implacable honesty, and the unassimilable scandal of evil?

I suspect that there is no general answer to that: we simply have to examine one theology after another and see whether we find it. I think Isabel Wollaston is right, that this is a decisive matter for the possibility of theology. Even if we find it, however, there is no guarantee that others will recognize it where we do. So we are back in the situation of reciprocal testimony. I want to end with such testimony to two theologians who have helped to make theology possible for me.

Donald MacKinnon died in March 1994. He was perhaps the greatest British Christian theologian of this century. The main reason is that he embodied what it is to wrestle as a philosophical theologian with the evil of this century, not least the Holocaust. In a commemorative lecture in Cambridge, George Steiner (who has wrestled with similar questions and was a close friend of MacKinnon) spoke of a perception of the reality of incarnate evil which verged on the Manichaean, together with a passion for precise remembering. Steiner (who, if such labels are to be risked, would probably be called an agnostic Jew) also gave a careful, powerful description of MacKinnon's attempt to think the resurrection of Jesus Christ after Auschwitz. Here, in a testimony growing out of this friendship, was something like an answer to Isabel Wollaston's question.

Donald MacKinnon was one of Frances Young's teachers. I see her work, especially in relation to her handicapped son Arthur,[7] as offering a variation on similar sombre themes. There is the wrestling year after year, the attention to narrative detail, and the sense of being drawn inexorably into further dimensions of Gethsemane, the crucifixion and the resurrection. It results in something very important for what Isabel Wollaston calls 'the theological enterprise': not just her own books, lectures and various public roles, but also the shaping of a department of theology as the sort of public forum where all the lectures published in the present book have a place.

Notes

1. See above, Chapter 8.
2. Edith Wyschogrod, *Spirit in Ashes: Hegel, Heidegger and Man-made Mass Death* (New Haven and London: Yale University Press, 1985).
3. See Frances M. Young, '*Paideia* and the myth of static dogma' in Sarah Coakley and David Pailin (eds), *The Making and Remaking of Christian Doctrine. Essays in Honour of Maurice Wiles* (Oxford: Clarendon Press, 1993), pp. 265–83; and '*Paideia* – what can we learn from the first four centuries?', to be published in David Ford and Dennis Stamps (eds), *Essentials of Christian Community. Festschrift for Daniel W. Hardy* (Edinburgh: T. & T. Clark).
4. Paul Ricoeur, *Oneself As Another* (Chicago and London: University of Chicago Press, London, 1992).
5. Eberhard Jüngel, *God as the Mystery of the World: On the Foundation of the Theology of the Crucified One in the Dispute between Theism and Atheism* (Edinburgh: T. & T. Clark, 1983).
6. See above, note 16 to Chapter 6, p. 88.
7. See especially the 2nd edition of Frances M. Young, *Face to Face* (Edinburgh: T. & T. Clark, 1990).